VEGETARIAN KITCHEN

SARAH BROWN

BBC PUBLICATIONS

This book accompanies the BBC Television Series
Vegetarian Kitchen, first broadcast on BBC2
from early summer 1984

Producer and book editor: Jenny Stevens
Food adviser and food preparation: Elaine Bastable
Photographs: Robert Golden
Stylist: Antonia Gaunt
Illustrations: Ray and Corinne Burrows

I would like to thank my friends, staff and assistants
at both The Terrace Project and the Vegetarian Society
for their help in preparing recipes for this book.
Grateful thanks, too, to Sue Buckley for the many hours spent
typing the manuscript, to Caroline Walker for her expert advice on
nutrition and to Glyn Davies who designed such an attractive and
clear layout for the book.

Published to accompany a series of programmes
prepared in consultation with the
BBC Continuing Education Advisory Council

Published by BBC Publications
a division of BBC Enterprises Ltd
35 Marylebone High Street, London W1A 4AA
ISBN 0 563 21034 6 (paperback)
ISBN 0 563 21095 8 (hardback)

Typeset in 11/13 Monophoto Century Schoolbook
Printed in England by Jolly & Barber Ltd, Rugby, Warwickshire
Bound by Chorley and Pickersgill Ltd, Leeds, Yorkshire
Cover printed by Belmont Press, Northampton

CONTENTS

CONVERSION TABLES

All these are *approximate* conversions, which have either been rounded up or down. In a few recipes it has been necessary to modify them very slightly. Never mix metric and imperial measures in one recipe; stick to one system or the other.

Weights

$\frac{1}{2}$ oz	10 g
1	25
$1\frac{1}{2}$	40
2	50
3	75
4	110
5	150
6	175
7	200
8	225
9	250
10	275
12	350
13	375
14	400
15	425
1 lb	450
$1\frac{1}{4}$	550
$1\frac{1}{2}$	700
2	900
3	1·4 kg
4	1·8
5	2·3

Volume

1 fl oz	25 ml
2	50
3	75
5 ($\frac{1}{4}$ pint)	150
10 ($\frac{1}{2}$)	275
15 ($\frac{3}{4}$)	400
1 pint	570
$1\frac{1}{4}$	700
$1\frac{1}{2}$	900
$1\frac{3}{4}$	1 litre
2	1·1
$2\frac{1}{4}$	1·3
$2\frac{1}{2}$	1·4
$2\frac{3}{4}$	1·6
3	1·75
$3\frac{1}{4}$	1·8
$3\frac{1}{2}$	2
$3\frac{3}{4}$	2·1
4	2·3
5	2·8
6	3·4
7	4·0
8 (1 gal)	4·5

Measurements

$\frac{1}{4}$ inch	0·5 cm
$\frac{1}{2}$	1
1	2·5
2	5
3	7·5
4	10
6	15
7	18
8	20·5
9	23
11	28
12	30·5

Oven temperatures

Mark 1	275°F	140°C
2	300	150
3	325	170
4	350	180
5	375	190
6	400	200
7	425	220
8	450	230
9	475	240

INTRODUCTION

Why am I a vegetarian? It all started six years ago when I opened a small wholefood shop stocking some of my favourite things such as muesli and brown rice. I became curious about other items which customers were asking for. What exactly were adukis, kombu and tahini? I felt that if I was going to stock these things I ought to find out more about them, and my love of cooking led me to experiment with these and other ingredients, making different dishes and creating combinations of foods which were unusual to me then. I found how much I enjoyed this way of eating and it suited both my lifestyle and my conscience, so eventually I changed to a vegetarian diet.

I think vegetarianism must always have been in my subconscious because before I opened the shop I had always been squeamish about eating meat or fish as it made me think of the living creature from which it had come. Since this rather simplistic beginning I have learned a lot more about the whole philosophy of vegetarianism and its sense has much appeal for me.

At this point I will define my terms as they can be a little confusing. A vegetarian is someone who does not eat any products derived directly or indirectly from the slaughter of animals, fish, or birds. This includes such by-products as gelatine, aspic and lard. Such vegetarians are referred to as lacto-vegetarians. A vegan takes this one stage further by not eating any product which involves the exploitation of animals. This diet excludes all dairy products and eggs as well as flesh, fish and fowl and, in some cases, honey as well.

A wholefood diet need not necessarily be vegetarian or vegan. Wholefoods are foods to which nothing has been added or taken away. This diet is primarily concerned with health, since it is believed that foods which retain as much of their natural goodness as possible, and are not processed or refined are better for us.

Since I've become vegetarian, I've had to cope with many different reactions from people when they find this out, ranging from the hairdresser who, while he had me firmly pinned under the dryer, insisted on describing the comforts and luxuries afforded to battery hens (he knew the local factory farmer intimately, of course) to the comment overheard at a vegetarian buffet I gave recently: 'It couldn't have been real brandy in that gâteau, you know; I mean, she's vegetarian, isn't she?'. It all goes to show how muddled people are about it.

Individuals decide to become vegetarian for many different reasons. For many vegans and vegetarians the argument focuses on the plight of animals, not only those which are slaughtered for food, but also those which are exploited by factory farming methods or used for experimentation. In general people are rather ignorant of the abuse which animals suffer. Farming is a very competitive business, and the methods adopted are those which cut costs and increase production. Under the conditions standard on modern poultry farms, for example, four hens may live out their lives in a cage with a floor area only the size of a tabloid newspaper. Experimenting on animals is a major industry as well with over 4,443,843 experiments performed in 1981, for example. How many of these experiments had no direct or urgent purpose? Is it possible to find methods of research which do not involve animals? Certainly the outcry over unnecessary experimentation has led some members of the cosmetic industry to develop products without involving cruelty to animals.

Then there are the three E's — economy, ecology and environment. We could use our land to much greater advantage by producing vegetable protein for direct human consumption rather than feeding it to beef cattle for us to get the protein second-hand. It takes 20 lb of vegetable protein to produce 1 lb of meat protein. About 80% of the world's agricultural land is used for feeding animals and 20% for feeding man directly. Huge amounts of grain are imported from under-developed countries to feed cattle. The world food problem could be eased if these products were available as food for the populations which produce them.

Another reason for adopting vegetarianism as a way of life is concerned with health. Many common British diseases could be prevented by eating a diet which at least leans in the direction of vegetarianism. A diet containing more cereal foods — rice, wheat, barley, corn, rye, etc. — would be particularly beneficial at least as far as our colons are concerned. About 40% of the population think they are constipated and about 20% regularly take laxatives. The consumption of larger quantities of less refined cereal foods would solve the problem in the vast majority of these cases.

Research clearly indicates that a diet high in saturated fat — the sort found in large amounts in dairy fats, meats and some vegetable oils such as palm and coconut oils — is a contributory cause of heart disease. Vegetarian diets are traditionally quite low in saturated fat, although some British vegetarians do eat quite a lot of milk and cheese. Cutting out meat from the British diet would remove, on average, a third of all the fat we eat, much of it saturated. It would of course be replaced by other foods, but the ensuing diet is unlikely to contain as much saturated fat as before, as long as too much emphasis is not placed on full-cream milk and high-fat cheeses. Comparisons of vegetarian and non-vegetarian communities in the USA and Europe suggest that vegetarians have less heart disease, less intestinal disorders and better teeth. In general we tend to be a healthier group of people!

If you have decided to opt for a wholly vegetarian way of life you should pay some attention to balancing the nutritional content of your meals. There are four main vegetarian food groups:

    beans and nuts

    grains

    dairy produce

    fruit and vegetables.

If you eat something from each of these groups every day, you will be sure of getting all the nutrients you require.

There are many who will never be complete converts to vegetarianism but who enjoy eating vegetarian-style often. I hope this book will help such people explore some of the many delights of vegetarian cookery and extend their repertoire of vegetarian dishes.

PREPARATION

When you are trying any new cuisine it takes a while to adjust, but vegetarian cookery is basically very easy. It contains its own range of quickly prepared dishes as well as more elaborate ones. With vegetarian meals, much can be prepared in advance. Many dishes improve with re-heating or will keep a day or so in the refrigerator. Some of the recipes may take a little time to prepare but they are then cooked in the oven and virtually look after themselves.

EQUIPMENT

There are one or two items of equipment which will help you save time. The vegetarian cook doesn't really need any special utensils though an electric grinder or mill, or food processor is extremely useful for pulses, as is a liquidiser for blending soups and making vegetable purées. A pressure cooker is also a tremendous help in cutting down the cooking times for beans and grains, and for making soups.

It is true there is a fair amount of chopping to be done when using so many vegetables. I think a large knife is essential as you can obviously chop more ingredients, more quickly. It is generally safer too, since the blade has more weight and depth and is less likely to slip. Always chop using the part of the knife that is near the handle as this way you have more control.

SHOPPING

The majority of ingredients used in this book are available in large supermarkets, good greengrocers, health food stores and wholefood shops. It is wise to build up a small store-cupboard as some ingredients do need soaking or cooking in advance. But as most of the pulses, grains, flours and dried fruits all keep from three months to up to a year, there's little danger of them becoming stale. Having said that, I don't think it's worth rushing out to buy a mass of new ingredients. It's best to pick a couple of recipes at a time, buy in for those, use the ingredients and familiarise yourself with them.

FRESH FOODS

Buy fresh vegetables as much as possible and get the best value by buying in season. The recipes in this book cover a wide range of vegetables so you should always be able to pick a dish for which the ingredients are in season. Although I've suggested certain vegetables, there aren't any hard and fast rules about substituting one vegetable for another.

FREEZING

Many of the recipes in this book will freeze satisfactorily. Take care when freezing spicy food or dishes heavily flavoured with garlic as these can spoil. Some dishes with a substantial amount of dairy products do not freeze well. If you freeze something like a vegetable stew I think some of the texture and appearance is lost when it is reheated. In that case I think it is best to cover it with a crisp pastry topping or savoury crumble as this greatly improves its appearance.

Cooked beans freeze very well and it is useful to have a few different types ready in the freezer. When they are cooked, drain them, put them into a container and shake once or twice as they freeze so that the beans don't stick together. Then take small amounts off the top as you need them.

TIME-SAVING TIPS

I think you'll find, as I certainly have, that a vegetarian style of life is just as quick and easy as the traditional ways of eating. Here are a few time-saving tips to help you when you are first starting out.

SOUPS AND STARTERS

If you have no stock on hand to make soup, simply mix water with a little soy sauce or tomato purée and add a bay leaf.

The quickest cooking pulses for soups are red lentils, continental lentils and aduki beans. None of these need soaking overnight so you can cook them straight away.

In general, soups freeze very well. If they are heavily spiced or contain a lot of garlic, don't keep them frozen for too long or the flavour will spoil.

Grapefruit or avocado make good starters when you are in a hurry and can be converted into something more elaborate if served with a dressing.

Most pâtés can be prepared ahead of time.

MAIN COURSES

🐝 Choose a rice or other grain dish which can be cooked in one pot such as a paella or risotto. Grains do not need soaking and rice, millet and buckwheat cook in less than 30 minutes.

🐝 If you want to make a bean dish, remember to soak the beans the day before or use the quick-boil method. Always cook a few more than you need as left-over beans are very useful for salads, pâtés or puréeing into soups.

🐝 If you choose a dish which involves quite a lot of vegetable preparation, then pick a simple accompaniment such as rice or pasta that needs little preparation.

SALADS

🐝 Simple green salads are very quick to assemble. Don't feel that a salad has to be a mass of different ingredients. Two or three vegetables can make a very effective combination.

🐝 If you are having a light main course then your salads can be more substantial. Use a grain or bean as these can be cooked well in advance and improve with keeping, particularly a marinaded bean salad or a tabbouleh.

🐝 Vinaigrette dressing can be prepared in advance and stored in the refrigerator. Use that or plain yoghurt to make a salad more interesting.

PUDDINGS

🐝 A choice of fresh fruit is lovely either served alone or with cheese.

🐝 Fruit crumbles are very quick to make. The toppings can be taken from a rubbed-in pastry mix which will freeze well. For the filling use some dried fruit and you'll find it will cook in about half an hour.

ENTERTAINING and MENUS

When cooking was my hobby, one of my greatest pleasures was to invite people for a meal. Now I run a restaurant I entertain on a large scale, cooking a range of dishes to make a tempting meal for people eating out. It's no problem to find exciting vegetarian food for special occasions. As with all entertaining, much depends upon how the food is presented. Soups can be enhanced with a garnish. Casseroles or baked pasta dishes look more exotic when cooked in individual pots. Flans, pizzas and salads can make a stunning display for a cold buffet. Roasts can be baked in all sorts of shapes to add more interest and can be served with more elaborate sauces. I think it's also interesting to give a meal a theme. With vegetarian cookery, as ideas are drawn from around the world, you can easily have, for example, Mexican, Italian or Indian evenings.

'What do you eat at Christmas?' is a question any vegetarian is always asked. Well, I start with a special soup such as Cream of Tomato with Sage, and follow this with Winter Vegetable Pie, Brussels sprouts, roast potatoes and Somerset Glazed Carrots, perhaps accompanied by Mushroom and Sherry Sauce and Onion Sauce, and of course I end with Christmas Pudding. One year, though, I tried something more oriental and covered the table with all sorts of different dips, relishes and salads, omelettes cut into tiny shreds, rice salads and bean sprouts. I improvised a wok arrangement in the centre of the table and each guest took a share in cooking their vegetables. It was great fun.

When planning a party menu try to choose dishes which contrast in colour, texture and choice of ingredients, and select courses with an eye to the overall amount of preparation time required. If your starter is an elaborate one, pick a main course which entails less work. Overleaf are just a few ideas for menus to suit different occasions:

FAMILY SUPPERS

Red Dragon Pie	Caponata
Savoury Brown Sauce	Vegetable Lasagne
Steamed Broccoli	Mixed Green Salad
Fruit Salad	Stewed Fruit

Lentil Croquettes with Parsley Sauce	Cheese Potatoes with Caraway
Buttered Spinach	Crisp Green Stir-fry
Baked Potatoes	Classic Tomato Salad
Fruit Crumble	Brown Bread Ice-cream

LUNCH PARTIES

Cream of Pea Soup with Tarragon	Melon with Grapes and Port
Stuffed Courgettes	Italian Fennel Casserole
Brown Rice	Rice Salad with Herbs
Lettuce Salad	Cinnamon and Carrot Cake
Pears Alhambra	

Avocado with
Blue Cheese Dressing

French Onion Tart

Ratatouille

Apple, Carrot and
Sunflower Seed Coleslaw

Blue Poppy Seed Cake

COLD BUFFET

Cream of Pea Soup with Tarragon	Stuffed Cucumber Rings
Roulade Chatelaine	Asparagus Flan
Apple, Carrot and Sunflower Seed Coleslaw	Tabbouleh
Greek Bean Salad	Summer Salad
St. Clement's Cream Cheesecake	Apricot Syllabub

COCKTAIL SAVOURIES

Sesame Sablés

Falafels

Cornbread Muffins with
Cheese Board

Rich Bread Ring Stuffed with
Almonds and Poppy Seeds

Spring Salad Tomatoes

Miniature Lentil Croquettes

Creole Pâté on
Wholewheat Canapés

Crudités with:
Yoghurt and Tahini Dip
Blue Cheese Dressing
Tofu Mayonnaise

DINNER PARTIES

Eggs Florentine	Mushroom Bisque
Chilli Bean Casserole	Red Cabbage Ragout
Flemish Salad with Tofu Dressing	Mixed Green Salad
Mixed Green Salad	Savoury Beans with Cream and Parsley
Pears Alhambra	Baked Potatoes
	St. Clement's Cream Cheese Cake

Tahini Dip with Crudités	Pears in Cream Dressing
Curried Eggs	Layered Cashew and Mushroom Roast
Summer Salad	Mushroom and Sherry Sauce
Spiced Vegetable Pilau	Broccoli in Lemon Cream Sauce
Apricot Syllabub	Roast Potatoes
	Carob and Orange Roulade

Stuffed Soufflé Tomatoes

Buckwheat Pancakes
filled with Ratatouille

Cheese and Fennel Coleslaw

Blue Cheese Dressing

Mixed Green Salad

Rum and Raisin Cheesecake

INGREDIENTS

Most of the ingredients in this book will be very familiar to you. Grains and pulses play an important part in vegetarian cookery and I have described these individually in the prefaces to the chapters devoted to each of these. Here is a short description of some of the other ingredients used where there may be some confusion.

BEAN SPROUTS

Bean sprouts are useful salad ingredients as they can be grown at any time of the year. They are especially good with crunchy vegetable salads or with rice salads such as the Oriental Rice Salad (page 186). If you want to grow your own bean sprouts for this salad it is very easy and you need very little equipment. They are especially good value in winter as other salad ingredients can then be quite expensive.

Types of sprouts
Sprouts can be grown from grains, vegetables or pulses. Mung beans and alfalfa seeds (lucerne) are probably the best choice for beginners as they grow quickly and have an excellent flavour. Grain and vegetable sprouts need no cooking, but sprouts from peas and beans should be cooked for a short time to make them more digestible. Grain sprouts are lovely when kneaded into bread dough or added to breakfast muesli. Bean sprouts are most often used in oriental cooking especially in stir-frys with other vegetables. Vegetable sprouts are a tasty addition to salads and add crunch to sandwich fillings.

How to grow sprouts
Sprouts can be grown in a variety of containers, but drainage is essential. The simplest method is a wide-necked jar with a porous cover such as muslin, but colanders, fine sieves or mesh trays can be used instead.
1   Pick out any sticks, stones or damaged seeds and wash the beans or seeds thoroughly.

2   Put two tablespoons of beans or seeds into a jar and fill it up with lukewarm water and leave this to stand overnight. This soaking process helps break down the outer shell so that the growth is quicker.

3   Next day, pour off the water and leave the jar in a warm place. If sprouts are grown in the dark they will contain more vitamin B2. If they are grown in the light there is more vitamin C and chlorophyl.

4   Every night and morning, until the sprouts are ready, rinse the seeds in the jar with lukewarm water. Shake them gently so as not to damage the delicate sprouts and drain them thoroughly. It's best to turn the jar upside down so that all the excess water drains away as if too much moisture is left, the sprouts may go rancid. Most sprouts take about four days to grow and grow to about $1\frac{1}{2}-2$ inches. Then they will keep fresh for four to five days in the refrigerator.

CHEESES

Most hard cheeses are set with rennet, which is usually derived from an animal source, and are therefore not strictly vegetarian. Cheeses made with vegetable rennet are becoming increasingly available, however, and can usually be found, labelled as such, in health food shops. There is a hard Swiss cheese, called Geska or Schabseiger, which is made without rennet and which is ideal for grating. It is a good alternative to Parmesan cheese.

Soft cheeses such as cottage or curd cheese tend to have a much lower fat content than hard cheeses. They usually contain rennet but those made with vegetable rennet can be found in health food shops.

DRIED FRUITS

Dried fruits contain the goodness of fresh fruit in a concentrated form. They are a rich source of protein, vitamins and minerals. There are many types available and they store well. Keep them in air-tight containers in a cool cupboard and they should keep for up to a year. The dried vine fruits are currants, raisins and sultanas. The dried orchard fruits available are dates, figs, prunes, peaches, apricots and apples. All dried fruits can be used for baking, muesli, sauces, salads, puddings and snacks.

The fruits can be used as they are or soaked first and stewed gently in water or fruit juice. Generally I find it is better value to soak or stew the fruits as they will then double or treble in size and weight. Although dried fruits are very nutritious they do contain a high proportion of sugar and it is wise to remember that if you eat them raw you are eating them in a concentrated form. (NB If you want to chop up dried fruit, to add to muesli for example, try using a pair of kitchen scissors.)

JELLING AGENTS

Vegetarians eschew gelatine and aspic because they are derived from the bones or flesh of animals or fish. Vegetable jelling agents are used instead, such as carrageen, which is basically a seaweed. The most commonly used product, however, is agar–agar. Agar–agar is made from a sea vegetable or seaweed and has been used in Japan since the 16th century where it was used for making jelly and ice-creams. The word comes from the Malay word for jelly.

In this country agar–agar can be bought in stick, flake or powder form. Powdered agar is the most common and you can buy it quite easily in wholefood stores or health food shops. It is superb for setting jellies (use two level teaspoons per pint (570 ml) of liquid) and can also be used to make a dark glaze for savoury roasts, or garnishes (e.g. bay leaves) by boiling it in water coloured with yeast extract. In order to set, agar–agar has to be boiled, so if you want to use it in a cold soufflé or mousse, you must work out the total liquid quantity in the recipe. Measure out sufficient agar–agar to set the entire volume, then boil this with some or all of the liquid ingredients (see individual recipes). For example, in an apricot soufflé, use the apricot purée as the medium for boiling the agar–agar. I think it's worth trying.

NUTS AND SEEDS

There is a wide range of nuts and seeds, which play an important part in the vegetarian diet as they are high in protein and fats and provide a good variety of vitamins and minerals. Nuts and seeds can be used in many forms — blanched, roasted, chopped, flaked or ground. Nuts, particularly walnuts, cashews and brazil nuts, provide flavour and texture in savoury or salad dishes and are often used as the basis of a nut roast. Almonds, cashews and hazelnuts are particularly good in sweet dishes. Spreads and butters may be made from peanuts, sesame or sunflower seeds. Chopped nuts and seeds make good toppings for biscuits, crumbles and salads. Nut milks are more unusual and are made from ground cashew nuts or ground almonds mixed with water. A good substitute for cream can be made by making a nut milk, sweetening it with honey and thickening it with cottage cheese.

It's best to buy nuts loose rather than pre-packed as they are generally cheaper and fresher. Look for good quality nuts that are crisp and free from blemishes. As many recipes only require 1–1½ oz (25–40 g) per person a small amount goes a long way and so, used carefully, they are not expensive. Prices do fluctuate according to season so it's wise to look around and buy the best value at the time. Don't hoard them; all types of nuts are best used quickly.

To blanch nuts: simply cover them with boiling water and leave them for 3 minutes; the skin will then rub off easily.

To roast nuts: either lightly oil a frying-pan and toss the nuts over a gentle heat for 5 to 10 minutes until they are an even colour, or spread them out on a baking tray and put them into a moderate oven gas mark 4, 350° F (180° C) for 10–15 minutes, shaking the tray occasionally until the nuts turn an even brown colour.

Tahini

Tahini is another name for butter made from sesame seeds. Light or dark brown tahini is available from health food shops and Greek delicatessens. It has a smooth consistency and a taste not unlike peanut butter. Dark tahini has a stronger flavour than the light variety. When mixed with water, tahini becomes thicker and can then be added to vegetable purées to make a dip, or mixed with honey for a sweet spread.

OILS AND FATS

Fats are solid at room temperature, whereas oils are liquid. Most people in Britain are thoroughly confused about the different kinds of oils and fats which are now available. Here is a simple guide.

Saturates, monounsaturates and polyunsaturates

Chemists divide the components of oils and fats into these three categories, according to their molecular structure. The details need not concern us but the important thing to know is that fats and oils containing a lot of *saturated* fat are harmful if eaten in large quantities. Conversely, fats and oils which contain a lot of *polyunsaturated* fat may be beneficial. Monounsaturates occur in all fats and oils and have a neutral effect on blood, i.e. they appear to do neither harm nor good. Olive oil is high in monounsaturates.

The British diet contains a large quantity of saturated fat, which is nowadays deemed to be unhealthy as it increases our risk of getting heart disease. Dairy fats (cream, butter, milk and cheese), beef and lamb are particularly high in saturated fats. So are palm and coconut oils. Any vegetable oil that is artificially hardened to make margarine or biscuit filling, for example, becomes more saturated and therefore more harmful. Even some soft margarines actually contain a lot of saturated fat. Therefore, being vegetarian doesn't automatically mean you're healthier since some vegetarians eat quite large quantities of milk and cheese. Do not assume either that a liquid 'fat', i.e. oil, is automatically better for you than a solid one as some blended or mixed vegetable oils are actually quite highly saturated.

What to use

The following fats and oils are good sources of polyunsaturates at the same time as being low in saturated fat:

Oils

Corn (maize) oil Corn or maize oil is compressed from the grain of corn or maize. It is light and easily digested with a rather bland flavour and is mostly used for frying.

Olive oil Though high in monounsaturated fat, some people find the price of olive oil somewhat prohibitive. It has a distinctive flavour, however, and I think it essential in certain dishes, particularly those of Mediterranean origin.

Safflower oil Safflower oil is a pale-coloured oil with a very delicate flavour. It combines well with olive oil to make a light salad dressing and can also be used for frying.

Sesame oil Sesame oil is extracted from sesame seeds and is used mainly in Chinese and Far Eastern cookery in salad dressings or sprinkled over cooked vegetables as a type of garnish. It has a strong, individual flavour so use it sparingly.

Soya oil Soya oil comes from soya beans. It is better used for frying than salad dressings since it leaves a slight after-taste.

Sunflower oil Sunflower oil is extracted from sunflower seeds. It is a pale yellow colour and is suitable for frying and for salad dressings as it has a pleasant flavour and light quality.

Walnut oil Walnut oil is generally used for salad dressings either in place of, or mixed with olive oil. It is particularly suitable for spinach salad. It is a highly flavoured oil and is usually very expensive.

Fats

Margarine Margarine may be made of either animal fats or vegetable oils. Look for a brand which is labelled 'high in polyunsaturates' as, confusingly, this means it is low in saturated fats.

Other Fats
There are two other fats which you will sometimes need in vegetarian cookery. Both of these are high in saturated fat so where
possible try to limit how much you use.

Butter Butter, which is made from cream, contains roughly 80%
milk fat with salt and colouring added. If you find it hard to abandon
butter in cooking, try using half butter and half oil; the oil will also
prevent the butter from burning.

Solid vegetable fats These are an alternative to lard which is made
from animal fats. There are many brands now available in supermarkets and health food shops. However, they are not as good
as oils from the health point of view as in order to make vegetable
fats solid they undergo a process known as hydrogenation which
changes the unsaturated fats into saturated fats.

SEASONINGS
Salt and pepper are our most common seasonings both during cooking and at the table, but vegetarians also place great emphasis on a
whole range of herbs and spices, including the Japanese or Chinese
condiments known as soy sauce (shoyu) and miso.

Miso
Miso is a by-product of fermented soya beans. It is a savoury brown
paste which is high in protein and which adds a rich flavour and
aroma to food. It can be used as a seasoning like salt although you
can't just sprinkle it on food in the same way. Instead dissolve it
first in a little hot liquid and then add it to the main dish. Miso can
also be used to make a quick stock for soup or can be mixed with
other ingredients to make sauces, dips and dressings. It can be obtained from good health food stores.

Pepper
Black peppercorns come from the unripened berries of the pepper
plant which when picked are green. As they dry out in the sun, they
turn a darkish brown-black. As peppercorns lose their flavour and
aroma fairly quickly once they are ground, it is best to use them
whole, grinding them freshly each time you need to flavour food.

Salt
Salt is a mineral which is essential to our diet though we only need
it in very small amounts. Most vegetables and dairy products contain

21

quite large traces of salt which is why you will find as you eat more of these products that you need to use less salt in your cooking. Salt is either mined from the earth or evaporated from the sea. Natural salts sold under the labels of *rock salt* or *sea salt* come in coarse or fine crystals and do not contain additives which is why many health conscious people prefer to use them. *Table salt* is basically rock salt but contains additives to keep it free flowing.

Soy sauce
Soy sauce is, like miso, also made from a natural fermentation of soya beans. It is often referred to as shoyu or tamari. It is a versatile condiment, containing valuable vitamins and minerals. It is widely used in oriental cooking or sprinkled over a cooked dish. Do not add salt to dishes containing soy sauce as the soy itself contains a lot. Soy sauce is readily available in most supermarkets, delicatessens and health food shops.

Yeast extract
Yeast extract is a highly flavoured brown substance which is made from a mixture of brewer's yeast and salt. It can be used to flavour casseroles and stews, or dissolved in water to make a stock or hot drink. Spread on bread or crackers it makes a tasty snack. Yeast extract is usually sold in a screw-top jar and will keep for up to six months.

SWEETENERS
Our consumption of refined sugar has risen steadily over the last century. It is important from a health and fitness point of view to cut it down. Many people think sugar is essential for energy. However, *all* food supplies energy, whether it comes in the form of fats, protein, starch or other carbohydrates, so it is quite unnecessary to eat sugar hoping that it will give you extra zest for life. When your blood sugar is low, body-fat stores (of which most of us have too much) are mobilised to restore the balance.

White and brown sugar
Many people buy brown sugars in the hope that they are more healthy than white. These include *Barbados sugar*, *molasses sugar*, *muscovado sugar*, *demerara sugar*, *Scotch moist* or *light raw cane sugar*. The country of origin should be printed on the packet, otherwise it is possible that it may only be a caramelised or dyed white sugar. 'Natural' sugars vary in colour from beige to dark brown and have a

better and stronger flavour. This means you are likely to use less. Brown sugar has slightly more minerals and vitamins but is really no better for you than white sugar because both rot your teeth and are equally unhelpful to the waistline.

Honey
Honey contains some vitamins and minerals. It consists of a mixture of glucose and fructose which is more easily assimilated by the body than sugar (sucrose). Its main advantage over sugar is that it is about twice as sweet. So when you're using honey in place of sugar in a recipe, cut down the amount you use by about half.

Fruit juice concentrates
There are a range of fruit juice concentrates now on sale in whole-food and health food shops. Apple and grape are the most common and they contain no additives or preservatives. They make excellent sweeteners for cakes, puddings and fruit salads and they can also be diluted to make drinks which are a good alternative to over-sugared soft drinks. The undiluted fruit juice keeps up to four weeks in the refrigerator but once diluted should be used within two days.

Molasses
Molasses is a by-product of the sugar-refining process. It is also known as 'black strap' molasses. Molasses has a very strong flavour and you do need to take that into account when substituting it for honey or sugar. It is particularly suitable for flavouring fruit and malt breads or ginger parkin as it gives a delicious moist quality and distinctive flavour.

VEGETABLES
Vegetables are useful sources of vitamins, minerals and fibre, but the amount of nutrients they provide will vary according to their freshness and the soil in which they are grown. So choose vegetables which look fresh. In general fruit and vegetables have a higher vitamin content if their colour is dark.

Preparing and cooking vegetables
Prepare and cook vegetables to preserve as much of the goodness as you can. Only peel fruit and vegetables if the skin is tough or blemished as the outer layers contain most of the vitamins. Cook the vegetables as soon as they are prepared in only a small amount of water. Soaking will draw out the valuable water-soluble vitamins.

When cooking vegetables, steam, grill or bake them, or, if you must boil them, always put them in water which is already boiling and don't add bicarbonate of soda because that destroys vitamin C. Vegetables should be firm when cooked and not water-logged.

Vegetables can be used as side or main dishes. If you are making a mixed vegetable dish, use an interesting combination of colours, flavours and textures, and if you have chopped a lot of vegetables for a meal, accompany it with something that needs very little preparation such as pasta, brown rice or bread.

Soups

Stock ❧ Bortsch ❧ Carrot and Orange Soup
Brown Lentil Soup with Lemon ❧ Pennsylvania Chowder
Minestrone Soup ❧ Creamed Tomato Soup with Sage
Leek Brotchan with Lemon and Parsley
Cream of Pea Soup with Tarragon ❧ Mushroom Bisque ❧ Harrira

Home-made soups are delicious and there is a tremendous range of flavours, colours and textures which can be created from vegetables, grains and pulses. Most soups are extremely easy and cheap to prepare, will freeze well and re-heat satisfactorily. Steaming hearty soups are just the thing in cold weather, and chilled soups are wonderfully refreshing in summer. Pick a thick soup such as Minestrone, add some bread, cheese and a couple of salads and you will have a wholesome lunch or supper. Soups don't always have to be basic fare, however, and I've included in this chapter some ideas for entertaining. When selecting a soup as a starter remember to pick one which will contrast or complement the main course. And don't give too large a portion or you will not be able to do justice to the rest of the meal!

Many vegetarian soups require stock. The basic recipe for this (opposite) consists only of vegetables, water and seasoning, but the liquor left from cooking many pulses is also very suitable as a stock for soup. Like soup, it can be made in large quantities and frozen.

Soups benefit from garnishing. Use a swirl of either cream or yoghurt in a creamed or puréed soup. Then sprinkle chopped parsley, watercress, paprika or sesame seeds on the top to add an interesting texture. A thin slice of tomato sprinkled with basil looks attractive floating in a pea or bean soup, and slices of hard-boiled egg or a little raw onion are delicious with lentils. Croûtons made from cubes of stale bread baked in a hot oven or fried lightly in some butter until they are crisp and brown are also delicious added to soup at the last minute. It really is worth taking those extra few seconds to make your soup look a little more attractive.

STOCK

Making vegetable stock isn't quite the time-consuming chore you might think. All you have to do is to scrub some vegetables, chop them into large chunks, fry gently with a few herbs, add some water and then you can forget it! Just leave the whole lot to simmer away for a couple of hours. I use root vegetables, particularly carrots and potatoes, with onions and celery. Adding parsnips gives a nuttier, sweeter taste, but avoid green vegetables such as cabbage, broccoli or Brussels sprouts as they can give stock rather too strong a flavour.

One of the best stock recipes I have ever tried suggested adding a whole head of garlic to the water. The end result was superb, leaving a subtle, almost imperceptible flavour. I've passed this idea on to many disbelievers and gained many converts.

4 potatoes
2 carrots
1 large onion
1 stick celery
1 tablespoon oil (preferably olive oil)
1 bay leaf
1 sprig fresh thyme or $\frac{1}{2}$ teaspoon dried thyme
$2\frac{1}{2}$ pints (1·4 litres) water
1 head of garlic (optional), peeled

Scrub all the vegetables and skin the onion, then chop them all into large pieces. Fry the vegetables very gently in the oil and add the herbs. If you want a pale stock do not let the vegetables colour.

Next add the water (and garlic, if using), bring to the boil and allow to simmer for $1\frac{1}{2}$–2 hours in a covered pan. Then strain and reserve the liquid for stock. The stock will keep 3–4 days in the refrigerator or it can be frozen. The remaining vegetables can be puréed and used for a thick soup or as the basis for a sauce.

BORTSCH

There are many recipes for this famous Russian soup but the main ingredient is always beetroot and the garnish is generally sour cream. The colour and flavour of the soup are superb, and the texture can either be coarse, or smooth if you purée it in a liquidiser. But do serve it chilled, with lots of sour cream.

Serves 4

12 oz (350 g) uncooked beetroot, peeled
6 oz (175 g) turnip or carrot, scrubbed
1 large onion, peeled and finely diced
$\frac{1}{3}$ pint (190 ml) tomato juice
$\frac{2}{3}$ pint (380 ml) stock or water
1 teaspoon caraway seeds (optional)
salt, freshly ground black pepper and nutmeg

Garnish:
$\frac{1}{4}$ pint (150 ml) soured cream

Prepare the vegetables and grate them coarsely. Then put them into a 3 pint (1·75 litre) pan with the tomato juice, stock and caraway seeds. Bring them to the boil, cover and simmer for 45–50 minutes. Season to taste with salt, pepper and nutmeg. Either leave this as a coarse soup or purée it in a liquidiser or mouli. Chill thoroughly and just before serving garnish with a swirl of soured cream.

CARROT AND ORANGE SOUP

This is a recipe I save for my travels as I can't yet buy fresh coriander locally, but thanks to a surge of interest in ethnic cookery in this country it is becoming much more readily available. If you cannot obtain coriander, use fresh parsley though this cannot really be called a substitute as it has such a different flavour.

The wonderful thing about carrot soup is that it is cheap and blissfully simple to make. It thickens when liquidised and has a beautiful rich colour. It is important to liquidise it thoroughly to obtain a smooth consistency and if you want something creamier, cook the carrots in less water, adding a little milk or cream after liquidising. I've also sneaked in a little sherry when I've been feeling extravagant.

Serves 4–6
2 tablespoons oil
1 medium onion, peeled and chopped
2 lb (900 g) carrots, scrubbed and chopped
1¾ pints (1 litre) light vegetable stock
½ teaspoon nutmeg
½ teaspoon paprika
1–2 tablespoons fresh coriander, finely chopped
rind and juice of 1 large orange
salt and freshly ground black pepper
Garnish:
extra coriander leaves
orange slices

Heat the oil in a pan, add the onions, then cover the pan and sweat them for 2–3 minutes. Peel and chop the carrots finely and add these to the pan. Cover again and sweat the vegetables for a further 10 minutes. Next add the stock, spices, coriander and the rind and juice of an orange. Bring to the boil and simmer for 40 minutes.

Let the soup cool, then liquidise it thoroughly, making sure it is completely smooth. Season it well with salt and freshly ground black pepper, then return the soup to a clean pan and re-heat it gently. You can serve this soup garnished with extra coriander or thin slices of orange.

29

BROWN LENTIL SOUP WITH LEMON

This is a rich brown soup with an interesting combination of spices and a delicious lemon tang. It is also quick and easy to make. This soup would be good followed by some sort of cheese dish or a quiche, salad and baked potato.

Serves 4
4 oz (110 g) small brown lentils
1 teaspoon oil (preferably olive)
2 pints (1·1 litres) water
1 bay leaf
1 tablespoon oil
1 large onion, peeled and finely chopped
1 clove garlic, crushed
1 teaspoon ground coriander
1 heaped teaspoon ground cumin
$\frac{1}{4}$ teaspoon paprika
1 large carrot, scrubbed and diced
2 sticks celery, chopped
juice of $\frac{1}{2}$ lemon
1 teaspoon grated lemon peel
salt and freshly ground black pepper

Pick the lentils over for stones and then rinse them well. Heat 1 teaspoon of oil in a saucepan and fry the lentils for a few minutes, stirring constantly, as this gives them a better flavour. Pour in the water, bring to the boil and add the bay leaf. Cover the pan and simmer for 30 minutes. Drain and reserve the cooking liquid for stock.

Next, heat the oil in a large pan, and add the chopped onion, garlic and spices. Fry the mixture gently for a few minutes. Add the carrot and celery, frying for a few more minutes and turning them over frequently so that all the vegetables get coated with the spices.

Add the cooked lentils and $1\frac{1}{2}$ pints (900 ml) stock. Bring to the boil, then simmer, covered, for 40 minutes. Add the lemon juice and grated peel and season to taste. Let the soup cool and then liquidise it. Return it to a clean pan and re-heat for 5 minutes. Serve straight away.

PENNSYLVANIA CHOWDER

Chowders are thick creamy soups made from a milk or cream sauce base with plenty of vegetables to add flavour and colour. This recipe is simple to make and colourful to look at with its bright sweetcorn and parsley. Milk-based soups should not be overcooked or the flavour will spoil, so once this soup is hot, serve it straight away.

Hearty soups of the chowder clan need little to accompany them, so I just dust on paprika to spice up the flavour. You could serve this one with Melba toast or crisp crackers.

Serves 4–6

1 pint (570 ml) vegetable stock
1 medium onion, peeled and finely chopped
4 sticks celery, washed and finely chopped
2 medium potatoes, scrubbed and diced
8 oz (225 g) sweetcorn, tinned or frozen
$\frac{1}{4}$ teaspoon paprika
1 oz (25 g) fresh parsley, finely chopped
1 pint (570 ml) milk
salt and freshly ground black pepper

Garnish:
paprika

First bring the stock to the boil in a large pan and add the onion, celery and potato, then simmer for about 10 minutes. Add the sweetcorn and paprika and cook for a further 10 minutes on a gentle heat. Then stir in the parsley.

In a separate pan bring the milk to the boil. Then pour this into the corn and vegetable soup. Purée half the mixture in a liquidiser and stir it back into the remaining mixture. Then re-heat the whole soup gently and season generously with salt and pepper. Pour into bowls and garnish with a dusting of paprika.

MINESTRONE SOUP

Minestrone soup is a rich thick soup which is always popular. It looks particularly attractive because it is full of different, colourful vegetables. It's easy to make and keeps well in the refrigerator.

Serves 4–6
1 small onion
1 clove garlic
2 sticks celery, chopped
1 tablespoon oil (preferably olive)
1 × 14 oz (400 g) tin of tomatoes, liquidised
1 bay leaf
$\frac{1}{2}$ teaspoon dried oregano
2 teaspoons fresh basil or 1 teaspoon dried basil
$\frac{1}{2}$ teaspoon fresh rosemary or $\frac{1}{4}$ teaspoon dried rosemary
3 oz (75 g) green pepper, de-seeded and diced
3 oz (75 g) carrot, diced
$1\frac{1}{2}$ pints (900 ml) stock
2 tablespoons tomato purée
1 oz (25 g) noodles, spaghetti or short cut macaroni
1 teaspoon salt
1 dessertspoon soy sauce
freshly ground black pepper to taste
1 tablespoon fresh parsley, chopped

Gently fry the onion, garlic and celery in the oil in a large saucepan for 10 minutes to soften them. Then add the tomatoes, herbs, vegetables, stock and tomato purée. Bring the soup to the boil and simmer it for 40 minutes in a covered pan. Then add the noodles, salt, soy sauce and pepper and simmer uncovered for about 15 minutes. Stir in the parsley and serve immediately.

OPPOSITE:
Minestrone Soup (*above*)
Leek Brotchan with Lemon and Parsley (*page 36*)
Carrot and Orange Soup (*page 29*)
Rich Bread Ring (*page 219*)

CREAMED TOMATO SOUP WITH SAGE

This recipe uses the basic stock (page 27) which is then transformed by a few ingredients into a deliciously rich cream soup. Although a lot of garlic is used in the stock, the end result has a mild flavour which gives the overall tomato taste a special quality. It is more subtle than you would expect. I find this soup makes a perfect starter for special meals since it is rich without being heavy.

Serves 4–6

1½ pints (900 ml) basic stock *with* garlic cloves
12 oz (350 g) tomato purée
1 teaspoon fresh sage leaves, chopped or ½ teaspoon dried sage
¼–½ tablespoon brown sugar
1 tablespoon red wine vinegar
1 tablespoon soy sauce
2 tablespoons sweet sherry
½ pint (275 ml) single cream or milk
salt and freshly ground black pepper

Garnish:
4–6 tablespoons soured cream or yoghurt
fresh sage leaves or sprigs of parsley

Make up 1½ pints (900 ml) of basic stock (see page 27) and include 6–12 cloves of garlic. Simmer the stock for 30 minutes, then strain. Dissolve the tomato purée in the stock and add the sage, sugar, vinegar, soy sauce and sherry. Bring this to the boil and simmer for 10 minutes, stirring occasionally. Let the soup cool slightly, then pour in the milk or cream. Season well and re-heat gently. Serve hot garnished with a swirl of cream or yoghurt and sprigs of parsley or fresh sage leaves.

OPPOSITE:
Crudités with Aioli (*pages 45, 202*)
Melon with Grapes and Port (*page 53*)
Pears in Cream Dressing (*page 51*)
Wholewheat Bread (*page 211*)

LEEK BROTCHAN WITH LEMON AND PARSLEY

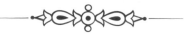

Brotchan is an Irish word for broth and is usually made from leeks, potatoes and other vegetables. I make this version adding butter beans which gives it an especially creamy texture. These are not so good to eat on their own as they can be bland but they purée beautifully, making a very delicate-coloured soup. Beans go particularly well with lemon and parsley, which give this soup a subtle flavour. I like to serve it with a choice of crackers spread with cream cheese and sprinkled with chives.

Serves 6–8
5 oz (150 g) butter beans
2 pints (1·1 litres) water for soaking
2 pints (1·1 litres) water for boiling
3 leeks
2 oz (50 g) butter
1½–2 pints (900 ml–1·1 litres) light stock (the water left after cooking the beans can generally be used here)
1½ oz (40 g) fresh parsley, finely chopped
juice of ½ lemon
1 tablespoon white wine vinegar
salt and freshly ground black pepper
Garnish:
4 tablespoons natural yoghurt or single cream

Soak the beans in water overnight, then drain and rinse well. Bring them to the boil in fresh water and boil rapidly for 10 minutes in order to destroy any toxins on them. Then partially cover the pan and simmer for a further 40–45 minutes or until the beans are fairly soft. When cooked, drain them and reserve the stock for use later.

Wash and slice the leeks. Melt the butter in a saucepan and cook the leeks gently for 4–5 minutes. Then add the beans and cook for a further 5 minutes, stirring occasionally. Add the stock and simmer in a covered pot for 20 minutes, then stir in the parsley. Allow the soup to cool slightly, purée and return to a clean pot. Re-heat the soup gently adding lemon juice and vinegar to taste depending on how sharp a flavour you like. Season generously with salt and freshly ground black pepper. You will probably find that you need to use quite a lot of salt. Pour the hot soup into bowls and garnish each serving with a tablespoon of natural yoghurt or cream.

CREAM OF PEA SOUP WITH TARRAGON

There's a magical flavour about fresh peas and for me it brings back memories of summer days as a child podding peas in the garden. Nowadays, of course, sweet tender peas can be bought frozen and this soup can be made all year round. It is a light, rich one that is simple to make, and the combination of cream, peas and tarragon is delicious hot or chilled. If you can't get fresh tarragon, then a good quality dried tarragon would do, or you could use mint.

Serves 6
1 bunch spring onions
3 oz (75 g) butter
1 lb (450 g) fresh, shelled or frozen peas
$\frac{1}{4}$ pint (150 ml) water
1 pt (570 ml) milk or single cream
1–2 teaspoons fresh tarragon or mint
salt and freshly ground black pepper

First clean the spring onions, then chop the white and green parts finely and reserve some of the green pieces for garnish. Melt the butter in a medium-sized saucepan on a gentle heat and add the peas, finely chopped spring onions and water. Cook until the peas are tender, which takes about 20–25 minutes. Let this cool slightly and then stir in the milk or cream and fresh tarragon. Season well with salt and pepper.

Put the soup into a liquidiser and liquidise until smooth. Then return it to a clean pan and re-heat gently. When serving, garnish each portion with the remaining chopped green spring onion.

MUSHROOM BISQUE

Mushrooms play an important role in vegetarian cookery as they have a good flavour and colour. Also, because they absorb other flavours, they can give a richness to many recipes, as well as being delicious in their own right. Flat mushrooms will make the soup dark, and button mushrooms will give it a paler colour.

Serves 6
3 oz (75 g) butter or oil
1 large onion, peeled and finely chopped
$\frac{1}{2}$ teaspoon salt
12 oz (350 g) mushrooms, button or flat
1 teaspoon dried dill
$\frac{1}{2}$ teaspoon dried thyme or 1 teaspoon fresh thyme
1 tablespoon paprika
$\frac{1}{4}$ teaspoon cayenne
1 pint (570 ml) dark vegetable stock
$\frac{1}{4}$ pint (150 ml) soured cream
salt and freshly ground black pepper
3 teaspoons fresh lemon juice
Garnish:
extra soured cream

Gently heat the butter or oil and fry the onion for 10 minutes adding $\frac{1}{2}$ teaspoon of salt while it is frying to bring out the juices. Meanwhile wipe and quarter the mushrooms, then add these to the pan with the dill, thyme, paprika and cayenne. Cook slowly for a further 7–10 minutes on a low heat, covering the mixture with some buttered paper and a lid. This extracts a great deal of flavour from both the onion and the mushrooms and also draws out juices which improve the final quality of the soup.

Pour in the stock and bring to the boil, then reduce the heat and simmer for 3 minutes. Cool slightly and then liquidise. Add salt and pepper and return the soup to a clean pan adding both the soured cream and lemon juice. Heat through but do not let it boil otherwise the cream will curdle. When serving, swirl in a little extra soured cream into each bowl.

HARRIRA (MOROCCAN SOUP)

Claudia Roden is an expert on Middle Eastern cookery which is rich in vegetarian dishes. This is her recipe for the national soup of Morocco which is traditionally prepared during the 30 fasting days of Ramadan, the important Moslem religious festival. In Morocco the perfume of harrira permeates the streets long before sunset when, at the sound of a cannon, the daily fast can be broken.

Serves 8

2 oz (50 g) chick peas
2 oz (50 g) butter beans
2 oz (50 g) black-eyed beans
2 oz (50 g) red kidney beans
2 oz (50 g) large green lentils
2 oz (50 g) yellow split peas
2 oz (50 g) green haricot beans
14 oz (400 g) tin peeled tomatoes
8 oz (225 g) onions, coarsely chopped
$\frac{1}{4}$ teaspoon black pepper
1 teaspoon turmeric
$\frac{1}{2}$ teaspoon powdered ginger
1 teaspoon cinnamon
juice of $\frac{1}{2}$ lemon
$1\frac{1}{2}$ teaspoons salt
$1\frac{1}{2}$–2 tablespoons flour
1 large bunch of fresh coriander or parsley, finely chopped
a few sprigs of mint, finely chopped, or 2 teaspoons dried mint
1 teaspoon paprika
a good pinch cayenne (optional)
2 oz (50 g) tiny pasta shapes or rice (optional)

Pick over and wash the pulses if necessary. Put the first two types in a large saucepan with plenty of cold water. Bring them to the boil, simmer for 2 minutes, turn off the heat and leave them to soak for an hour. Then drain the beans and put them back in the saucepan with 2 pints (1·1 litres) of water and simmer them for $1\frac{1}{2}$ hours.

Add the rest of the pulses, onions, tomatoes chopped up small with their juice, pepper, turmeric, ginger, cinnamon and lemon, but not the salt (or the beans will take longer to cook). Boil fast for 10 minutes and then simmer for another hour. Add the salt when the beans are tender, and about 2 more pints (1·1 litres) of water.

Add 3 dessertspoons of cold water to the flour and mix it to a paste. Beat in a few ladlefuls of broth and pour this back into the soup, stirring vigorously. Continue to stir until the soup is bubbling again and has thickened without leaving any lumps. The flour gives the soup a texture which the Moroccans call 'velvety' and which they usually achieve by stirring in leavened dough left over from bread making. Simmer the soup until the beans are soft. Add the herbs, paprika and cayenne and, if you like, pasta or rice and cook for about 15 minutes until these are done. Add water if the soup is too thick.

STARTERS and SAVOURIES

Creole Pâté with Spiced Fruit Salad ❧ Caponata ❧ Crudités
Greek Dip ❧ Yoghurt and Tahini Dip ❧ Falafels
Stuffed Cucumber Rings ❧ Stuffed Soufflé Tomatoes
Pears in Cream Dressing ❧ Tomato Chartreuse
Melon with Grapes and Port

Starting with an appetiser is a way of relaxing into a meal. Time spent over a first course always seems to me to set the pace for an enjoyable, leisurely lunch or dinner.

There are literally hundreds of delicious vegetarian starters and I have only given a fairly small range in this chapter to provide you with some alternatives to soup. Many salads make excellent appetisers, as do small portions of pasta with a sauce, or individual servings of some vegetable dishes, such as Ratatouille (page 177).

Vegetarian pâtés may be new to many so I've included two recipes – one using nuts and lentils, and one using vegetables. Another idea is to cook beans until they are soft enough to purée and make into tiny savouries. Falafels, a Middle Eastern speciality, is one such dish, which is delicious hot or cold. If you want an impressive starter for a special dinner party, the Stuffed Soufflé Tomatoes not only have a light, delicate flavour, but also look spectacular.

CREOLE PÂTÉ WITH SPICED FRUIT SALAD

Red lentils are quick to cook and need no soaking. The only thing which takes a little time is picking them over for tiny pieces of grit or sticks. (Do this while the lentils are dry since after they are washed it is much harder to separate them.)

This pâté is made with a mixture of lentils and peanuts, which blend together very well. I have found it best to use some peanut butter as well as nuts to give the pâté a rich creamy texture. Don't expect this to resemble a meat pâté, as it has a light golden colour and a spicy, nutty flavour. If you want a *very* creamy version which is more suitable for spreading, increase the peanut butter and decrease the amount of ground peanuts. For a more crunchy loaf texture, do the reverse. I think the spiced fruit salad is an ideal accompaniment, but of course you could serve it with crackers, toast or vegetable crudités.

Serves 6

For the pâté:
4 oz (110 g) uncooked red lentils
$1\frac{1}{2}$ pints (900 ml) water
1 teaspoon oil (for cooking the lentils)
1 tablespoon oil
1 teaspoon ground cumin
$\frac{1}{2}$ teaspoon turmeric
$\frac{1}{2}$ teaspoon ground coriander
$\frac{1}{2}$ teaspoon mustard powder
8 oz (225 g) onions, peeled and finely chopped
2 tablespoons smooth peanut butter
juice of $\frac{1}{2}$ lemon
4 oz (110 g) ground roasted peanuts
salt and freshly ground black pepper
$\frac{1}{4}$ teaspoon chilli powder

For the spiced fruit salad:
1 fresh green chilli, de-seeded and finely chopped
3 tablespoons olive oil
2 teaspoons white wine vinegar
salt and freshly ground black pepper
4 slices pineapple, fresh or tinned, diced
1 red or green pepper, de-seeded and diced
1 banana, peeled and sliced
1 avocado, peeled and diced

Spread the lentils out on a plate and pick out any tiny stones or ungerminated seeds, then wash them well in a sieve under the cold tap. Put in a saucepan with the $1\frac{1}{2}$ pints (900 ml) water and bring to the boil, skimming off any scum that forms. Add a teaspoon of oil to stop the water boiling over and cook the lentils gently for 15 minutes until they are quite soft. If they are still moist, dry them out over a low heat, stirring constantly, until the mixture becomes fairly firm. Drain and set aside.

Heat the tablespoon of oil in a pan, add the spices and cook until you can smell a good aroma. This takes about 3–5 minutes. Then add the onion and cook gently for 10 minutes over a low heat, stirring occasionally. Add the cooked lentils and mix them in thoroughly. Transfer the mixture to a bowl and beat in the peanut butter, lemon juice and ground peanuts. Add salt, freshly ground black pepper and, if you want a hotter version, chilli powder to taste. The mixture will be fairly creamy at this point, but if you put it into a lightly oiled dish, it will firm up when chilled and can even be turned out if you are careful. Alternatively use an ice-cream scoop to serve out individual portions.

To make the salad, put the chilli into a bowl, then add the oil, vinegar and seasoning and stir vigorously with a fork. Toss the remaining ingredients in this dressing and chill for 30 minutes before serving with the pâté.

CAPONATA

I like recipes where the vegetables are cooked and then marinaded as the process of marination brings out a superb flavour. Also, though our chilly climate often makes me long for bowls of hot soup, I find that I frequently appreciate flavours better when the food is cold. Some of these marinaded vegetable dishes are Mediterranean in origin and there are many variations. This particular dish is rather like a ratatouille but has a slight tang to it as it contains a little vinegar and some sharp pickled garnishes. Once cooked it will keep in a covered container in the refrigerator for up to a week.

Serves 8 as a first course
2 lb (900 g) aubergines, unpeeled and cut into $\frac{1}{2}$ inch (1 cm) cubes
salt
$\frac{1}{4}$ pint (150 ml) olive oil
4 sticks celery, washed and finely chopped
1 medium onion, peeled and finely chopped
3 fl oz (75 ml) red wine vinegar
4 teaspoons demerara sugar
1 × 28 oz (800 g) tin of tomatoes
2 tablespoons tomato purée
12 black olives, halved and stoned
1 tablespoon capers
salt and freshly ground black pepper

Sprinkle the cubes of aubergine with salt, put them in a large sieve and leave to drain for about 30 minutes. This draws out any bitter juices. Rinse the cubes and pat dry with kitchen paper. Heat 3 tablespoons of the olive oil in a large frying-pan, add the finely diced celery and cook over a moderate heat for about 8–10 minutes. Then add the finely chopped onion and cook for another 8 to 10 minutes until both onion and celery are soft and lightly coloured. Transfer to a bowl with a slotted spoon.

Now add another 3 tablespoons of oil to the frying-pan and fry the aubergine cubes over a high heat. Only fry a few at a time so that the oil remains hot and the cubes don't absorb too much of it. Use extra oil if you find it necessary. Cook each batch of the aubergines for 5–7 minutes until soft and lightly browned, then return all the celery, onion and aubergine cubes to the pan and stir in the vinegar and sugar, tomatoes, tomato purée, olives, capers, salt and pepper. Bring this to the boil, then reduce the heat and simmer uncovered for 15 minutes, stirring frequently. Correct the seasoning and add a little extra vinegar if necessary. Transfer the mixture to a serving bowl and let it cool thoroughly.

When the mixture is well chilled, spoon it out into individual serving dishes. It looks particularly attractive arranged on a bed of lettuce, and served with some hot garlic bread. It can also be served as a side dish to accompany a main course.

CRUDITÉS

Crudités are raw vegetables served with dips, crackers, bread or cheese. Many vegetables are suitable for this, e.g. carrots, celery, cucumber, cauliflower, fennel, peppers, radishes and swedes. Choose three or four with contrasting colours and cut them into a variety of shapes. Cut carrots, celery and swedes into small matchsticks, cucumber and radishes into rings, divide cauliflower into florets, and slice fennel and peppers. The vegetables can be left plain, or dressed with a little Vinaigrette Dressing (page 201) or Oriental Dressing (page 205). Crudités also make a colourful display on a buffet table, or at a cocktail party, and are a good summer starter.

GREEK DIP

This dip is made with tahini, a sesame spread not unlike peanut butter. It is sold by the jar and can be bought from wholefood shops, health food stores and Greek delicatessens. You can buy a dark tahini which is made from whole sesame seeds but I find this too strong and prefer the white or pale tahini which is made from hulled sesame seeds and is more delicate in flavour. Tahini tastes much better when watered down as this makes the flavour milder and the texture creamier and a little goes a long way. Once you develop a taste for it, you'll find it both delicious and versatile. This is a pale, creamy, smooth-textured dip and is particularly suitable for crudités.

Serves 4
2 tablespoons tahini
2 tablespoons water
juice of 1 lemon
1 tablespoon oil
2 teaspoons soy sauce

Mix the tahini with the water in a small bowl. Don't worry if at first it looks as though the mixture is curdling, because the natural oil in the tahini will not blend immediately with the water and it seems to form threads in the water. After a few seconds of stirring, however, the two ingredients will blend into a smooth cream. Add the other ingredients and season to taste.

YOGHURT AND TAHINI DIP

This is a variation on the previous recipe and makes a creamier sauce for salads or as a dressing for freshly steamed cauliflower.

Serves 4
1 recipe of Greek Dip (opposite)
¼ pint (150 ml) natural yoghurt
1 clove garlic, crushed
1 bunch spring onions, finely chopped (optional)
1 tablespoon parsley, finely chopped (optional)

Make up the Greek Dip, then mix in the yoghurt and garlic and let the mixture stand for 15 minutes so the flavours blend. Then stir in the finely chopped spring onions and a tablespoon of fresh, finely chopped parsley if using. Serve at room temperature.

FALAFELS

These savoury patties or rissoles are a traditional recipe from the Middle East where they are known as either ta'amia or falafel. They can be made either with white broad beans, haricot beans or chick peas. Generally they are highly flavoured with a variety of spices and seasonings and are either shallow-fried or deep-fried.

I prefer to use chick peas for falafels as they have such a distinctive nutty flavour and a warm golden colour. I also prefer to cook them first as I think this way they are more digestible. The cooking time for chick peas can vary tremendously according to the origin and age of the crop but I find if you are going to grind the cooked beans in an electric blender then you need only cook them until they are fairly soft, which takes about 45 minutes. Obviously if you have to mash them by hand you must cook them for a lot longer.

It is important to coat the finished falafels in egg white and breadcrumbs because this gives them a strong shell and makes them very easy to fry. If you don't do this, you will find they tend to stick. The Middle Eastern style is to serve them with a cucumber and tomato salad and Yoghurt and Tahini Dip (page 46). They are delicious as an appetiser or, by serving them with bread and salads, you could turn them into a light lunch.

Makes 16–20 falafels

8 oz (225 g) uncooked chick peas
3 pints (1·75 litres) water for soaking
3 pints (1·75 litres) water for boiling
2 large onions, peeled and minced
2 cloves garlic
2 teaspoons ground coriander
2 teaspoons aniseed
2 teaspoons caraway seed
1 tablespoon fresh parsley
salt and freshly ground black pepper
$\frac{1}{2}$ oz (10 g) fresh yeast or $\frac{1}{4}$ oz (5 g) dried yeast
a few tablespoons of water
2 egg whites
4 oz (110 g) fresh breadcrumbs
oil for deep or shallow frying

Pick the chick peas over, wash them thoroughly and leave to soak in a large bowl filled with 3 pints (1·75 litres) water for at least 8 hours (preferably overnight). Then drain the peas, wash them again under a running tap and bring them to the boil in a pan of fresh water. Boil rapidly for at least 10 minutes, then turn the heat down and simmer until tender. (This will take from 45–90 minutes depending on the age of the chick peas.)

When they are soft enough to grind, drain off the liquid and grind to a fine powder in a mill or food processor, or put through a mincer. Mince the onion and the cloves of garlic. Put the chick pea powder into a large bowl and mix in the onion, garlic, spices, parsley, salt and black pepper. Crumble in $\frac{1}{2}$ oz (10 g) fresh yeast or use $\frac{1}{4}$ oz (5 g) dried yeast dissolved in a little warm water. Add just enough water to the mixture to form a very stiff paste, and leave until quite cold.

Form the mixture into small balls, dip each ball into egg white and roll in fresh breadcrumbs. Then repeat the procedure as a double coating forms a good shell around each falafel which will prevent it from falling apart during frying. Shallow-fry or deep-fry the falafels until crisp. Serve warm.

STUFFED CUCUMBER RINGS

In this recipe chunks of cucumber are stuffed with a delicious pâté made from aubergines. Aubergines are not for the faint-hearted, but their unique, strong flavour is a taste worth acquiring. Be sure to chill the pâté well because it firms up in texture when cold.

Serves 4
2 large aubergines
a little oil
1 oz (25 g) flaked almonds
1 small onion, peeled and finely chopped
1–2 cloves garlic, crushed
1 tablespoon fresh parsley, chopped
salt and freshly ground black pepper
1 cucumber
1 lettuce
1 lb (450 g) tomatoes

Garnish:
lemon wedges or shreds of lemon rind
parsley sprigs

Pre-heat the oven to gas mark 6, 400°F (200°C).

Slice the aubergines in half and rub a little oil lightly over the skin. Place them face down on a greased tray and bake for 1 hour. Leave them to cool. Then scoop out the insides and mash or liquidise the pulp with the flaked almonds, onion, garlic and parsley. Season well and chill thoroughly.

Cut the cucumber into 8 × 1 inch (2·5 cm) rounds. Scoop out the middle of each round to form a small case, being careful not to cut all the way through. Either leave the cases raw, or, if you prefer, blanch them in boiling water for 5 minutes. Fill the cucumber chunks with the pâté.

Line a serving platter with lettuce and edge this with tomato slices. Put the cucumber cases in the centre and garnish with lemon rind and parsley sprigs.

FED SOUFFLÉ TOMATOES

...l dish is very easy to prepare. I've served it as a starter and as a lunch or supper dish with brown rice and salad. When large Italian tomatoes are in season you only need one per person, but for most of the year when it is only possible to buy smaller tomatoes I serve two or three per person.

Serves 4
12 small tomatoes
salt
2 fl oz (50 ml) milk
4 oz (110 g) grated Cheddar cheese
1 clove garlic, crushed
2 eggs, separated
2 teaspoons fresh marjoram or 1 teaspoon dried marjoram
salt and freshly ground black pepper

Pre-heat the oven to gas mark 5, 375°F (190°C).

Cut a lid from the *base* of each tomato and keep to one side. Scoop out the seeds and flesh carefully with a spoon. (The flesh can be used in a soup or sauce.) Lightly salt the insides of the tomatoes and drain them upside down on a plate for about 15 minutes.

Meanwhile heat the milk in a double boiler until it is just warm. Add 3 oz (75 g) of the grated cheese, the garlic, 2 egg yolks, marjoram, salt and pepper and heat until the cheese melts and the mixture thickens slightly, stirring frequently. Remove the pan from the heat.

In a separate bowl, beat the egg whites until just stiff and fold into the cheese mixture. Spoon some of the mixture into each of the tomato shells and put the filled shells into a lightly oiled baking dish, making sure there is plenty of space for each tomato. Sprinkle them with the remaining cheese and top with the lids. Bake for about 20 minutes and serve immediately.

PEARS IN CREAM DRESSING

I love using this dressing on fruit as it makes such a subtle, elegant appetiser with the cream-coloured sauce masking fresh pears or peaches. It looks particularly cool and inviting if served on a bed of fresh lettuce. I have also cut the pears into slices and tossed them in the dressing to make a rich salad which I have found very popular.

Most types of pear can be used in this recipe, but I prefer Williams, Comice or Packhams. If you find the fruit is a little under-ripe, poach lightly in fruit juice, cider or wine. For a change use peaches when they are in season.

Serves 4
1 egg
juice of $\frac{1}{2}$ lemon
1 dessertspoon light brown sugar
4 tablespoons double cream
1 teaspoon fresh tarragon or $\frac{1}{2}$ teaspoon dried tarragon
2 large pears or peaches

Garnish:
4 lettuce leaves
mustard and cress, watercress or 1 oz (25 g) chopped walnuts

Beat the egg thoroughly with the lemon juice and sugar in a small bowl then place the bowl over a pan of very hot water. Heat the mixture over the hot water until it thickens, stirring constantly. (Use a wooden spoon to stir the mixture as a metal one will discolour the egg.) If you find the mixture is cooking too quickly simply re-move the bowl from the hot water and keep stirring until it cools slightly. Then you can proceed as before. When the egg mixture is thick, set it aside to cool. Lightly whip the cream, then fold in the egg mixture and tarragon.

Peel the pears, cut them in half and remove the core; if using peaches, peel, halve and stone them. Set each half on top of a lettuce leaf on a small plate, then spoon the cooled dressing over the top of the fruit and decorate with a little mustard and cress, watercress or a sprinkling of chopped walnuts. Serve chilled.

TOMATO CHARTREUSE

The Carthusian monks from Grenoble in France, who were vegetarians, invented the idea of setting combinations of vegetables, either hot or cold, in moulds, and they gave these dishes the name of their monastery – La Grande Chartreuse. For cold moulds the vegetables are set in jelly and for this I use agar–agar (see page 18). The powdered form is the most readily available and can be bought in wholefood or health food shops either loose or pre-packed. Use 2 teaspoons to 1 pint (570 ml) of boiling liquid.

Serves 8
1½ pints (900 ml) tomato juice
10 fl oz (275 ml) water
4 teaspoons agar–agar (or other vegetable gelatine)
juice of ½ lemon
1 teaspoon soy sauce
salt and freshly ground black pepper
3 oz (75 g) mixed gherkins, and black or green olives, sliced (reserving some for the garnish)
1 tablespoon capers
Garnish:
shredded lettuce
sliced gherkins and olives

Put the tomato juice, water and agar–agar in a pan, bring to the boil and stir for 2 or 3 minutes until the agar–agar has dissolved. Then remove the pan from the heat and season the liquid with lemon juice, soy sauce, salt and freshly ground black pepper. Dip 8 individual moulds or ramekins in cold water, pour a layer of jelly into each and leave to set. Then arrange some sliced gherkins, olives and capers on the top. Cover with more jelly and leave to set again. Keep alternating layers of gherkins etc. and jelly until all the jelly is used. Do remember to keep some gherkins and olives for decoration. Put the moulds or ramekins into the refrigerator to set. Just before serving stand the moulds in hot water for a couple of minutes, then turn them out onto small plates. If they don't turn out the first time, stand them in hot water again. Surround each mould with shredded lettuce, garnish with extra gherkins and olives and serve with brown bread and butter.

MELON WITH GRAPES AND PORT

When I first had melon and port in a restaurant, I was served nearly a whole melon. The top had been cut off and a hole the size of a wine glass had been scooped out, which was filled to the brim with port. It was a very alcoholic start to a meal. My version of this idea is less extravagant but more colourful and makes a change from the ubiquitous melon boat.

Serves 4
1 honeydew melon
8 oz (225 g) black grapes
3–4 tablespoons port
Garnish:
sprigs of fresh mint
orange or lemon slices

Cut the melon in half and remove all the seeds. Scoop out the flesh using a melon baller or a teaspoon. Wash and halve the grapes and de-seed them. Pile the melon shells up with a mixture of melon balls and grapes and sprinkle over the port. Chill thoroughly and garnish before serving.

MAIN COURSES

The largest chapter in this book is devoted to main courses as this is the point at which people new to vegetarian cookery often get stuck. Most people find it easy to make vegetarian soups and salads, and puddings too pose no problem, but the traditional main course in this country tends to be meat or fish with two vegetables, generally one green and the other potatoes. Although many vegetarian meals can be built around the same convention – a savoury nut roast, for example, with the usual vegetable accompaniments – I think it is rather limiting to think of meals only in this way. If you reconsider our conventional eating pattern you will find there are many main dishes which can be served with a new range of accompaniments. Try serving bean dishes with vegetables and rice, egg dishes with salad, and vegetable sauces are delicious with pasta.

Inspiration for vegetarian dishes comes from all over the world and no one culture serves food in exactly the same way. This chapter includes dishes drawn from many cooking traditions including Indian, Chinese and American. I have divided it into smaller sections so that you can easily find a particular type of main course.

CASSEROLES and ROASTS

Country-style Hot-pot ✿ Basque Ratatouille ✿ Cheese and Lentil Loaf
Layered Tomato Loaf ✿ Layered Cashew and Mushroom Roast
Three Layer Terrine ✿ Vegetables à l'Anglaise
Italian Fennel Casserole ✿ Red Cabbage Ragout

Casseroles are easy to make and look after themselves once they are in the oven. Generally they benefit from re-heating so you can make them well ahead of time. Casseroles look particularly appetising if they are served either in individual portions or in the centre of a platter and surrounded by a cooked grain, such as rice or millet, or by creamy mashed potatoes. A salad usually makes a pleasant accompaniment.

Nut roasts could possibly more correctly be called nut loaves and they must seem to be the most predictable dish in the vegetarian repertoire. They have survived over-exposure, however, because they are so delicious. Roasts needn't just be made from nuts. In this section you'll find a variety of recipes using mixtures of nuts and vegetables, or lentils. Don't feel you always have to cook these in a standard loaf tin. I often use a ring mould, for example, and serve the roast turned out with its centre filled with vegetables. I also think an accompanying sauce is essential with a nut roast. There are plenty of suggestions for these in the chapter on Sauces (page 149).

COUNTRY-STYLE HOT-POT

Chestnuts are so versatile that they can be used in either sweet or savoury dishes. They have a quality which is excellent for rich nut roasts and a warm dark colour when cooked which gives depth to casseroles, hot-pots and stews. Now that dried Italian chestnuts are available all the year round, it is possible to make such dishes in winter and summer.

For this casserole I've chosen vegetables which are of a similar size, such as button mushrooms, pickling onions and Brussels sprouts. These combine well with the chestnuts, which I like to leave whole, so that the stew is made of little chunky vegetables.

The cheese nuggets are a little like dumplings and can be made in a few minutes while the casserole is cooking. Serve this hot with mashed potatoes or mashed swede and parsnips, broccoli or braised leeks.

Serves 6

4 oz (110 g) dried chestnuts
2 pints (1·1 litres) water for boiling
½ lb (225 g) whole pickling onions
½ lb (225 g) carrots
½ lb (225 g) Brussels sprouts
4 oz (110 g) button mushrooms
1 tablespoon oil
½ teaspoon mustard powder
1 dessertspoon soy sauce
salt and freshly ground black pepper
2 tablespoons fresh parsley, finely chopped

For the cheese nuggets:
2 oz (50 g) fresh breadcrumbs
2 oz (50 g) grated Cheddar cheese
1 egg
¼ teaspoon salt
¼ teaspoon mustard
¼ teaspoon paprika

Bring the chestnuts to the boil in 2 pints (1·1 litres) of water. Cover the pan and simmer for 40–50 minutes until just tender. Drain and reserve the liquor. Meanwhile prepare the vegetables. Scald the onions in boiling water, then peel them, leaving them whole. Peel the carrots and slice into rings. Clean the Brussels sprouts and wipe the mushrooms.

Heat the oil in a flameproof casserole or large saucepan and gently fry the onions for a few minutes. Then add the carrots and mustard powder. Continue frying the vegetables on a low heat for a few minutes, turning them over in the oil. Add the soy sauce, cooked chestnuts and 1 pint (570 ml) of the liquid in which they were cooked. Bring to the boil and simmer for 30 minutes.

While this is cooking make the cheese nuggets. Mix together the breadcrumbs and grated cheese in a small bowl. In a separate bowl beat the egg and then mix it, together with the salt, mustard and paprika, into the breadcrumb and cheese mixture. Form the mixture into small balls the size of walnuts. After the hot-pot has cooked for 20 minutes, add the cheese nuggets, Brussels sprouts, mushrooms and parsley. Season to taste and continue cooking it for a further 15–20 minutes until the cheese nuggets are cooked and the Brussels sprouts are tender. Serve straight away.

BASQUE RATATOUILLE

Ratatouille was originally a French gypsy dish meaning a stew of vegetables and the different regions of France offer a variety of recipes bearing this name. Red peppers predominate in Basque cookery and they have a distinctive colour and flavour. This brightly coloured dish can be served with brown rice, pasta or potatoes to make a main meal, or it can be served as a side dish to accompany a flan or savoury bake.

Serves 4

½ lb (225 g) onions, peeled and finely chopped
2 tablespoons oil (preferably olive)
2 cloves garlic, crushed
1 lb (450 g) courgettes or marrow, washed and sliced
1 lb (450 g) tomatoes, skinned and chopped
1 red pepper, de-seeded and sliced
1 teaspoon parsley, chopped
salt and freshly ground pepper

Cook the onions and garlic very slowly in the oil for about 10–15 minutes so that they become juicy and translucent. Then add all the remaining ingredients and simmer with the lid on for about half an hour. Serve straight away.

CHEESE AND LENTIL LOAF

Red lentils are most useful in a vegetarian diet as they are quick and easy to cook and combine well with a whole variety of foods, giving dishes substance and colour. When cooking lentils for a purée, start with only a small amount of water and check after about 10 minutes of cooking to see how soft and moist they are. Add a little extra boiling water if necessary. In this recipe, you need quite a stiff purée, as the remaining moisture is provided by the eggs and cream. Serve this loaf with Tomato Sauce (page 154) and either baked potatoes and a green vegetable such as Broccoli in Lemon Cream Sauce (page 165), or with fried rice with grilled tomatoes.

Serves 4
6 oz (175 g) red lentils
12 fl oz (350 ml) water
4 oz (110 g) grated Cheddar cheese
1 onion, peeled and finely chopped
1 tablespoon fresh parsley, chopped
$\frac{1}{2}$ teaspoon cayenne pepper
a little lemon juice
1 large egg
3 tablespoons single cream
salt and freshly ground black pepper
1 teaspoon butter

Pre-heat the oven to gas mark 5, 375°F (190°C).

Pick over the lentils for any sticks and stones. Rinse thoroughly and cook in a tightly covered pan with the water for 10–15 minutes. Check after 10 minutes in case you need to add more water. The mixture should cook to a stiff purée. Remove the pan from the heat and mix in the grated cheese, chopped onion, parsley, cayenne pepper and lemon juice. Season to taste.

In a separate bowl lightly beat the egg, stir in the cream and then pour this mixture over the lentils. Grease a 1 lb (450 g) loaf tin with the teaspoon of butter and press in the mixture. Bake for 45–50 minutes until the top is golden brown and the mixture feels firm to the touch. If you are serving this loaf hot, let it stand for 10 minutes in the tin before turning it out. Alternatively, serve cold with a salad.

LAYERED TOMATO LOAF

This is a variation of the previous recipe with added colour and interest. It is especially good for a summer lunch or dinner party.

Serves 4

1 recipe Cheese and Lentil Loaf mixture (page 59)
1 lb (450 g) tomatoes, washed and sliced

Pre-heat the oven to gas mark 5, 375°F (190°C).

Make the loaf mixture following the basic recipe. Divide it into three and press one third into a greased 1 lb (450 g) loaf tin. Cover with a layer of sliced tomatoes. Repeat this procedure, finishing with a final layer of loaf mixture. Bake for 45–50 minutes. Serve either hot or cold.

LAYERED CASHEW AND MUSHROOM ROAST

Nut loaves and roasts are very popular in vegetarian cookery and can be particularly successful if dressed up a little, either by layering the basic mixture with vegetables, or by arranging decorative nuts or vegetables in the bottom of the tin before pouring the loaf mixture in. This gives you a design on the top of the loaf when you turn it out. I find greasing the tin with butter rather than oil makes it easier to turn the loaf out successfully.

This recipe is delicious hot served with Spiced Somerset Carrots (page 167), roast potatoes, a green vegetable and Mushroom and Sherry Sauce (page 158). Alternatively, serve it cold as part of a salad meal with a baked potato.

Serves 6–8

1 tablespoon of oil
1 small onion, finely chopped
2 cloves garlic, crushed
8 oz (225 g) cashew nuts
4 oz (110 g) fresh breadcrumbs
1 egg
3 medium parsnips, cooked and mashed with a little butter
1 teaspoon fresh rosemary or $\frac{1}{2}$ teaspoon dried rosemary
1 teaspoon fresh thyme or $\frac{1}{2}$ teaspoon dried thyme
1 teaspoon yeast extract
$\frac{1}{4}$ pint (150 ml) hot water or stock
salt and freshly ground black pepper
1 oz (25 g) butter
8 oz (225 g) mushrooms, chopped
butter for greasing tin

Pre-heat the oven to gas mark 4, 350°F (180°C).

Heat the oil and fry the onion and garlic until soft. Grind the cashew nuts in a nut mill, blender or mincer, then mix with the breadcrumbs. Beat the egg and add it to the dry ingredients, then mix in the mashed parsnips and herbs. Add the fried onion, being sure to scrape the pan so that all the juices go in as nut roasts can sometimes be a little dry. Dissolve the yeast extract in hot water or stock and add to the other ingredients. Season well.

Melt the butter in a frying pan and sauté the chopped mushrooms until soft. Grease a 2 lb (900 g) loaf tin with butter, then press in half the nut mixture. Cover with a layer of mushrooms and top with the rest of the nut mixture. Then cover with foil and bake for 1 hour. When cooked, remove the loaf from the oven and let it stand for 10 minutes before turning it out. Serve hot or cold.

THREE LAYER TERRINE

I find this terrine very popular as the ingredients are familiar to most people and it has a good crunchy texture. You can simply mix all the ingredients together but I think it is worth the extra effort to keep them separate and make a layered loaf as this looks much more attractive.

The terrine can be eaten either hot or cold, but when hot it is fairly crumbly so I tend to serve it straight from the dish. Bear this in mind when cooking it and bake it in something that you can bring to the table, such as an attractive, deep pottery pâté dish. If you do want to turn it out to serve it, you'll find it easier if you line the tin with foil or greaseproof paper. This terrine is delicious with Barbecue Sauce (page 156) and could be served with baked potatoes and Ratatouille (page 177).

Serves 4
2 oz (50 g) grated cheese
3 oz (75 g) fresh brown breadcrumbs
2 tablespoons oil
1 onion, peeled and finely chopped
2 sticks celery, finely chopped
3 oz (75 g) raw peanuts
2 oz (50 g) ground almonds
1 teaspoon fresh marjoram or ½ teaspoon dried marjoram
1 teaspoon fresh thyme or ½ teaspoon dried thyme
salt and freshly ground black pepper
14 oz (400 g) tin of tomatoes, drained
butter for greasing the dish

Pre-heat the oven to gas mark 5, 375°F (190°C).

Mix together the grated cheese and breadcrumbs in a large bowl and moisten them with 1 tablespoon of oil. Heat the remaining tablespoon of oil in a frying-pan and gently fry the onion and celery until fairly soft. Roughly chop the peanuts and add them to the frying pan along with the ground almonds and herbs. Mix together well and remove the pan from the heat. Season well. Liquidise or sieve the drained tomatoes.

Line and thoroughly grease a 1½ lb (700 g) loaf tin or deep pâté dish. Press in a layer of the cheese and breadcrumbs, then a layer of nuts and celery, then a layer of liquidised tomatoes. Repeat these layers, ending with a topping of cheese and breadcrumbs. Press down well. Bake for 1 hour or until firm to the touch. Serve hot or cold. If you want to turn the terrine out while it's hot, be sure to let it stand at least 10 minutes so that it firms up before removing it from the tin.

VEGETABLES À L'ANGLAISE

The term 'à l'anglaise' is usually defined as meaning 'cooked in a homely manner', a good description of this pie where the lightly cooked, colourful vegetables piled on top of a tasty cheese and potato crust have a simple but fresh appeal. It doesn't take long to make and can be adapted all year round according to what vegetables are in season. Serve with a cheese or tomato sauce and a side salad, or choose an accompanying vegetable which contrasts with those used in the pie, such as Buttered Spinach (page 179).

Serves 4
2 lb (900 g) potatoes, peeled
4 oz (110 g) Cheddar cheese
1 onion, peeled
2 tablespoons oil
salt and freshly ground black pepper
3 leeks, washed and finely chopped
1 lb (450 g) carrots, scrubbed and diced
1 small cauliflower, divided into florets
½ lb (225 g) mushrooms, wiped and sliced
2 tablespoons oil
2 teaspoons fresh parsley or rosemary
For the topping:
4 oz (110 g) grated cheese
1 tablespoon fresh parsley, finely chopped

Pre-heat the oven to gas mark 4, 350°F (180°C).

Grate the raw potatoes, cheese and half the onion by hand or in a food processor. Mix in 2 tablespoons of oil and season well. Press this mixture into a 9 inch (23 cm) deep pie-dish, building up the sides to form a shell. Bake in the oven for 45 minutes until the crust is just beginning to brown.

Meanwhile prepare the vegetables. Heat 2 tablespoons of oil and fry the remaining onion (chopped), leeks, carrots and cauliflower florets slowly for 5–10 minutes, turning them over in the pan. Then add the sliced mushrooms and continue cooking all the vegetables for a further 5 minutes with the pan covered. Add the herbs, salt and freshly ground black pepper.

Next pile the vegetables into the baked cheese and potato crust and sprinkle 4 oz (110 g) cheese mixed with 1 tablespoon chopped parsley over the top. Bake for 20 minutes until the edges of the shell look crisp and the cheese has melted. Serve hot.

ITALIAN FENNEL CASSEROLE

Culpeper's *British Herbal* published in 1652 says of fennel that 'most gardens grow it and it needs no description' but I think today fennel is unfamiliar to many people. Most fennel comes from Italy. It has a mild and refreshing aniseed flavour and is delicious raw, baked or braised. It makes an excellent casserole when prepared with tomatoes and garlic and I sprinkle over a light cheese and bread-crumb topping to give the dish a little substance.

Serves 4
1 lb (450 g) or 3 bulbs of fennel
2 tablespoons oil (preferably olive)
1 large onion, peeled and finely chopped
3 cloves garlic, crushed
14 oz (400 g) tin of tomatoes
salt and freshly ground black pepper
2 oz (50 g) fresh brown breadcrumbs
2 oz (50 g) grated Cheddar cheese

Pre-heat the oven to gas mark 6, 400°F (200°C).

First prepare the fennel by discarding any coarse outer leaves and the root base and slice the bulbs very thinly. Keep some of the feathery tops for a garnish. Heat the oil in a large pan and gently fry the chopped onion and garlic. Add the slices of fennel and cook these for a few more minutes, turning them over in the pan. Put the tin of tomatoes into a small bowl and break them down slightly with a spoon. (This makes them easier to stir into the fennel.) Add the tomatoes to the fennel and onion mixture and season well. Cover the pan and simmer for about 10 minutes, then transfer the vegetables to a lightly greased 3 pint (1·75 litre) ovenproof dish. Mix the cheese and breadcrumbs together and sprinkle over the top, then bake the casserole for 15–20 minutes until the top is nice and crisp. Serve immediately.

RED CABBAGE RAGOUT

Red cabbage is a splendid vegetable with a beautiful colour and flavour. It is very popular in many European countries, particularly Scandinavia, Germany and Austria. You can devise quite a number of variations on this theme by using either red wine or vinegar, and sugar, apples or raisins as the sweetening together with a variety of spices. Cook the cabbage in as little liquid as possible so that it cooks in its own steam. It will then be soft when cooked but without having lost its texture. This dish keeps well and will re-heat. It can be eaten hot or cold and is particularly good with potatoes or as a pancake filling, served with a little sour cream.

Serves 4
2 lb (900 g) red cabbage
1 tablespoon oil
2 onions, peeled and sliced into rings
2 dessert apples, washed and sliced
$\frac{1}{2}$ teaspoon cinnamon or whole caraway seeds
3 fl oz (75 ml) red wine or red wine vinegar
salt and freshly ground black pepper

Pre-heat the oven to gas mark 3, 325°F (170°C).

Remove any tough or wilted leaves on the outside of the cabbage then shred it finely using as much of the core as possible but discarding any tough pieces. Heat the oil in a large saucepan and gently fry the onion rings. After a few minutes add the apples and spice. Stir these in well and continue cooking for a few more minutes. Then add the finely shredded cabbage, the wine or vinegar, and 4 tablespoons of water. Stir these in well and then transfer the mixture to a lightly oiled 3 pint (1·75 litre) ovenproof dish. Cover it with a well buttered piece of greaseproof paper and a tight-fitting lid. Put it in the oven and cook it for 1–1½ hours, checking occasionally on the water content. This dish can also be cooked on a very low heat on the top of the cooker but if you do this, check it more often in case it catches on the bottom of the pan. When the cabbage is soft, season it well with salt and freshly ground black pepper and serve with sour cream.

OPPOSITE:
Vegetables à l'Anglaise (*page 63*)
Three Layer Terrine (*page 62*)
Red Cabbage Ragout (*page 65*)
Wholewheat Bread (*page 211*)

OVERLEAF:
Spaghetti with Green Vegetables in Cheese Sauce (*page 97*)
Spinach and Mushroom Lasagne (*page 101*)

EGGS

Roulade Chatelaine ❧ Spinach Roulade with Cheese Sauce
Cheese Soufflé ❧ Watercress Soufflé ❧ Curried Eggs
Spring Salad Tomatoes ❧ Piperade ❧ Eggs Primavera ❧ Eggs Florentine
Omelettes:
Spanish Omelette ❧ French Omelette ❧ Omelette Fines Herbes
Tomato Omelette

Eggs are a versatile food and a good source of protein. It's easy to turn a couple of eggs into a quick meal and I have often been served an omelette when people are stuck for a vegetarian idea. Some omelette recipes have been given in this section, but there are many other egg dishes which are just as quick to make, including such simple favourites as Curried Eggs and Eggs Florentine as well as more impressive dishes such as soufflés and roulades. Eggs, of course, need not always be the main part of the meal and many of the recipes here can be used to make tasty starters.

Most vegetarians eat eggs, although there are some, known as vegans, who eat no animal products at all. Battery production of eggs is nearly as cruel as factory farming methods for meat, however, so I always buy free-range eggs. I'm lucky enough to be able to go direct to the farm to collect them and be sure they really are free-range. If these are not available I prefer to do without eggs completely. As yet there aren't any satisfactory substitutes for eggs, although I have included a recipe for an egg-free cake in the Puddings and Cakes chapter (page 223). You can use tahini mixed with water instead of egg as a binding agent for a croquette or savoury roast (use about 1 tablespoon of tahini to replace 1 egg).

ROULADE CHATELAINE

A roulade is basically a soufflé which is cooked on a tray the size of a Swiss roll tin and then rolled up. If you do not have a suitable tin, you can easily make a tray out of folded greaseproof paper, holding the corners together with paper clips. Serve this elegant roulade for a special lunch or in small portions as an impressive starter for a dinner party. The idea of filling it with salad is unusual but delicious, and it takes very little time to prepare. I like to serve it with Rice Salad with Herbs (page 189) and a choice of green salads for lunch, or garnished with tomato wedges or watercress as a first course.

Serves 4 for a main meal, 6–8 as a starter
1½ oz (40 g) butter
1 oz (25 g) flour
½ pint (275 ml) warm milk
3 oz (75 g) Gouda cheese, grated
1 tablespoon capers, chopped
3 egg yolks
salt and freshly ground black pepper
3 egg whites
1–2 oz (25–50 g) Parmesan cheese

For the filling:
3 oz (75 g) cooked peas
6 oz (175 g) fresh, cooked or tinned asparagus
2 tinned artichoke hearts
3 tablespoons mayonnaise or a mixture of mayonnaise and sour cream

Pre-heat the oven to gas mark 6, 400°F (200°C).

Grease and line an 8 × 12 inch (20 × 30 cm) Swiss roll tin. Melt the butter in a pan, sprinkle in the flour and allow the roux to cook for 2–3 minutes. Then pour over the warm milk, stirring all the time and bring the sauce to the boil. Cook it for 5 minutes over a very gentle heat. Remove the pan from the heat and stir in the grated Gouda cheese and capers. Let the sauce cool slightly, then beat in the egg yolks and season well. Put it back over a gentle heat until it thickens, then allow to cool.

In a separate bowl beat the egg whites until they form soft peaks. Stir 1 tablespoon of whipped egg white into the sauce, then fold in the remainder. Spread the mixture evenly on the prepared tin and bake for 15 minutes until the roulade has risen and is firm to the touch. Remove from the oven and turn out onto a clean sheet of greaseproof paper sprinkled with Parmesan cheese and peel off the lining paper. Cover the roulade with a damp tea-towel to stop it drying out.

Meanwhile prepare the filling. Pat the peas, asparagus and artichoke hearts dry with kitchen paper, then mix them with the mayonnaise. Shortly before serving, spread this filling over the cooked roulade and roll it up. Use the greaseproof paper to help you and don't try to roll it too tightly. Serve it immediately.

SPINACH ROULADE WITH CHEESE SAUCE

This delicate roulade makes a light lunch dish or evening meal accompanied by a salad. It only takes 12–15 minutes in the oven and this particular recipe is easy to make as it is really just a matter of separating the eggs and combining them with the spinach.

Serves 3–4
1½ lb (700 g) fresh spinach
4 eggs, separated
pinch of nutmeg
salt and freshly ground black pepper

For the cheese sauce:
1½ oz (40 g) butter
1 oz (25 g) flour
½ pint (275 ml) warmed milk
4 oz (110 g) Cheddar cheese, grated
pinch of nutmeg
¼ teaspoon cayenne pepper
salt and white pepper
extra grated cheese for garnishing

Pre-heat the oven to gas mark 6, 400°F (200°C).

First prepare the spinach by washing it in several changes of water and then shaking off as much excess water as possible. Put into a heavy-based pan, without any water and cook quickly for 6–8 minutes. Then chop very finely.

Mix the egg yolks with the cooked spinach, and season with nutmeg, salt and black pepper. Whisk the egg whites in a separate bowl until they are moist in appearance and form soft peaks. Stir just 1 tablespoon of egg whites into the spinach mixture, and then fold in the remainder in 2 batches. Put this mixture into a lined and greased Swiss roll tin 8 × 12 inches (20 × 30 cm) and bake for 10–15 minutes until it is just beginning to brown.

Meanwhile prepare the sauce. Melt the butter over a gentle heat in a small saucepan, then sprinkle over the flour, and cook the roux for 2–3 minutes. Then pour in the warmed milk and, stirring constantly, bring the sauce to the boil. When it is boiling, let it simmer over a gentle heat for 5 minutes. Remove the pan from the heat and stir in the grated cheese and season with the nutmeg, cayenne pepper and salt and pepper.

When the roulade is cooked take it out of the oven, turn out onto a clean sheet of greaseproof paper and peel off the lining paper. Then spread some of the sauce over the top and roll the roulade up. Do this by first folding over a small edge of the roulade and then use the greaseproof paper sheet to ease it into a roll. Don't try to roll it too tightly and do expect it to crack slightly. Pour the remaining sauce over the top. Sprinkle with extra grated cheese and put the roulade back in the oven for 5–10 minutes until the cheese has melted and turned brown. Serve immediately.

CHEESE SOUFFLÉ

It is the fleeting perfection of a hot soufflé that makes it very special and it is because we tend to keep soufflés for special occasions that success with them is so crucial. As with many culinary processes, however, it is simply a matter of following a few guidelines and then success is assured.

A soufflé is made in two stages: the sauce, and the blending of egg whites. The sauce part of the soufflé is easy to master. For a cheese soufflé it is worth using a strong cheese such as Parmesan or Gruyère, but a mixture of these cheeses with Cheddar is also fine. A strong-flavoured cheese is necessary to counter-balance the blandness of the egg whites. Cheese contains a lot of salt so season carefully.

Make sure that the sauce is cool before folding in the egg whites or they will start cooking before the soufflé is in the oven. The egg whites should be beaten in a bowl that is free from grease or flecks of yolk. If beaten in a copper bowl they are stabilised by a chemical reaction which takes place between the albumen and the copper. If you don't have a copper bowl, a china or glass bowl is a good alternative.

Serves 4

1 oz (25 g) butter
1 oz (25 g) flour
½ pint (275 ml) warm milk
4 oz (110 g) grated cheese, preferably half Gruyère or Parmesan to half Cheddar
salt
freshly ground black pepper or cayenne pepper
4 egg yolks
4 egg whites

Pre-heat the oven to gas mark 6, 400°F (200°C).

Melt the butter in a small saucepan, mix in the flour and cook this roux for 3 minutes. Pour in the milk, stirring constantly and cook for 3–5 minutes, continuing to stir well. (Remember to scrape round the edges of the pan to beat in all the uncooked roux.) Remove the pan from the heat and stir in the mixed cheeses. In a separate small bowl thoroughly beat the egg yolks and then beat them into the warm sauce. Set aside to cool and then season carefully with a little salt, black pepper or cayenne pepper.

Beat the egg whites, preferably by hand, in a copper, china or glass bowl. When they look moist and velvety in appearance and are just standing in soft peaks, stir 1 tablespoon into the cheese sauce. Then fold in the remaining egg whites in 2 batches. For this use a palette knife or metal spoon and treat the mixture carefully. Remember that every cutting action breaks down the air in the egg whites which give the soufflé its characteristic quality.

Put the soufflé mixture into a buttered 1½ pint (900 ml) soufflé dish and bake for 25–30 minutes in the centre of the oven on a baking sheet. Try not to open the oven door until the end of the cooking time. The soufflé is cooked when it has risen well above the level of the dish and is golden brown and firm to the touch. If at the end of the cooking period it is still soft in the centre, leave it in the oven another 5 minutes. It should not deflate. Serve immediately as the soufflé will inevitably collapse about 5 minutes after it is taken out of the oven.

WATERCRESS SOUFFLÉ

Chopped watercress gives this soufflé a subtle peppery flavour and an interesting speckled appearance. Land cress is becoming a popular alternative to watercress and its leaves are even more fiery. I like to eat soufflés accompanied only by a salad and a glass of white wine.

Serves 4
1 oz (25 g) butter
1 oz (25 g) flour
$\frac{1}{2}$ pint (275 ml) warm milk
2 oz (50 g) Cheddar cheese, grated
$\frac{1}{2}$ teaspoon prepared mustard
4 egg yolks
salt and freshly ground black pepper
1 bunch watercress, very finely chopped
4 egg whites

Pre-heat the oven to gas mark 6, 400°F (200°C).

Melt the butter in a small saucepan, stir in the flour and cook the roux gently for 2 or 3 minutes. Pour in the warmed milk and bring the sauce to the boil, stirring constantly. (Remember to scrape round the edges of the pan so that all the uncooked roux is well stirred in.) When the mixture comes to the boil, let it simmer over a very gentle heat for 3–5 minutes, stirring occasionally. Then remove the pan from the heat and add the grated cheese and mustard. When the sauce has cooled a little, beat in the egg yolks and then season the mixture to taste. Remember that the cheese will already have made this sauce quite salty.

Add the chopped watercress to the sauce. In a china, glass or copper bowl beat the egg whites, preferably with a hand whisk, until they are moist and velvet in appearance and just peak softly. Then stir a spoonful of beaten egg white into the cooked sauce. Fold in the remaining egg whites in two batches, cutting the mixture through with a metal spoon or palette knife. Put this mixture immediately into a greased 1½ pint (900 ml) soufflé dish and bake as in previous recipe for 25 minutes or until it is well risen and firm to the touch in the centre. Serve the soufflé straight away.

CURRIED EGGS

Curry powder is familiar to most of us, but it is more interesting and more authentic to make up your own combinations of spices. As a guide-line, remember that the strength and colour of curry comes from chilli, cayenne, paprika and turmeric, and the flavouring comes from ginger, cumin and coriander. Try to buy spices from a shop where the turnover is quick so they are fresh. March and April herald the new season for spices, so if you feel yours are stale or you have had them quite a few months, it is a good idea to replace them at that time of year. Serve this dish with rice and a light green salad for a delicious supper.

Serves 3
4 medium onions, peeled
2 cloves garlic, crushed
4 medium tomatoes, skinned and chopped
4 oz (110 g) butter or oil
2 teaspoons ground coriander
1 teaspoon turmeric
1 teaspoon root ginger, freshly grated
2 teaspoons ground cumin
$\frac{1}{2}$–1 teaspoon cayenne pepper
1 teaspoon salt
6 eggs

Slice 2 of the onions finely and then chop the remaining 2 into fine dice. Heat the butter or oil gently in a frying-pan and add the onion slices. Fry these until golden brown and then add the remaining diced onions, garlic, tomatoes and spices. Cook this mixture for 25–30 minutes over a gentle heat.

Meanwhile prepare the eggs. Put them in a pan of cold water, bring to the boil and boil them for about 10 minutes. Then immediately crack them and put them into cold water to prevent a dark ring forming around the yolk. Shell them, cut in half, and place on top of the simmering sauce and to heat through for 5–10 minutes. Transfer to a serving dish and serve straight away.

SPRING SALAD TOMATOES

These tomatoes with their light filling make a delicious starter, or they can also be a complete meal served with a rice salad or baked potato. The combination of eggs, artichoke hearts and mushrooms mixed with fresh herbs and a little wine vinegar is delicious, and a dab of cream cheese on the top of the tomatoes not only secures the lid, but also adds a rich finish.

Serves 4
1 large egg, hard boiled
2 oz (50 g) mushrooms, wiped and sliced
$\frac{1}{2}$ oz (10 g) butter
2 artichoke hearts, tinned
$\frac{1}{2}$ tablespoon fresh parsley, finely chopped
salt and freshly ground black pepper
1 tablespoon white wine vinegar
8 medium tomatoes (a starter for 4 people) or 4 large tomatoes (as a main meal for 2 people)
1 oz (25 g) cream cheese

First boil the egg. Remember that when eggs are hard-boiled, they must be cracked and put straight away into cold water after they are cooked to prevent a dark ring forming between the yolk and the white. Next fry the mushrooms in the melted butter until they are just soft. Finely chop the artichoke hearts, parsley, egg and sautéed mushrooms, and put all the ingredients into a bowl. Season thoroughly and mix in up to 1 tablespoon of white wine vinegar. Slice the bottoms off 8 small tomatoes, if you are serving this as a starter for 4, or 4 large Italian tomatoes if you want to prepare a salad meal for 4 people. Reserve the bottoms for 'lids'. Scoop out the centres of the tomatoes, keeping the flesh and seeds for a sauce or stock. Then season the insides of the tomatoes with the salt and pepper and fill them with the vegetable and egg mixture. Dab a little cream cheese on the top of each one and replace the lids. Serve chilled.

PIPERADE

Piperade is a scrambled egg and vegetable dish that originated in the Basque region of France where use of the red pepper is a feature of their cookery. Different versions can be made based on this idea by flavouring the eggs with garlic, basil or parsley, and varying the vegetables. It can be eaten hot or cold. Do not allow the vegetables to become too juicy, or the scrambled egg effect is lost. This dish is delicious served with slices of toasted home-made bread with garlic or herb butter, and a green salad.

Serves 3–4
1 onion, peeled and finely chopped
2 cloves garlic, crushed
2 tablespoons oil (preferably olive)
2 green or red peppers, de-seeded and diced
4 tomatoes, roughly chopped
6 eggs
salt and freshly ground black pepper
fresh parsley, finely chopped

Cook the onion and garlic for 5 minutes in the oil, then add the peppers and tomatoes and cook for a further 5 minutes. In a separate bowl beat the eggs, then pour these over the cooked vegetables and mix them in until they are lightly scrambled. Season to taste and serve garnished with parsley.

EGGS PRIMAVERA

This is my version of a popular French dish, oeufs en cocotte, which simply means eggs baked in the oven in individual ramekin dishes. In this recipe, sautéed mushrooms and cream add extra flavour to this baked egg dish. Serve it with salads or a green vegetable for a light meal, or on its own as a starter.

Serves 4
4 oz (110 g) mushrooms, wiped and very finely chopped
1 oz (25 g) butter
4 eggs
4 tablespoons cream

Pre-heat the oven to gas mark 4, 350°F (180°C).

Sauté the mushrooms in butter for 5 minutes. Divide the mixture between 4 individual ramekin dishes. Then break an egg into each dish and cover it with a tablespoon of cream. Put the dishes on a tray in the oven and bake for 15–20 minutes, or until just set. Serve immediately.

EGGS FLORENTINE

One good thing about our damp climate is that we can grow very succulent spinach and it is such a useful vegetable for combining with eggs or cheese in a variety of dishes. One of the best of these is Eggs Florentine where the eggs are served on a bed of spinach topped with cheese. The eggs can be poached first but I think it's easier to break them into nests formed from cooked spinach and finish off the dish in the oven. This is lovely when eaten with garlic bread and Classic Tomato Salad (page 186).

Serves 4
2 lb (900 g) spinach
6 tablespoons double cream
salt and freshly ground black pepper
pinch of nutmeg
4 eggs
4 tablespoons Cheddar or Parmesan cheese, grated

Pre-heat the oven to gas mark 6, 400°F (200°C).

Wash the spinach several times, using fresh water each time. Then shake off all the excess water and put the spinach into a heavy-bottomed pan. Cover and cook gently in its own liquid for 6–8 minutes until tender. Squeeze out as much moisture as you can and chop it finely. Return the spinach to the saucepan and add the cream, salt, freshly ground black pepper and nutmeg. Stir this over a very gentle heat for 1 minute, then transfer to a lightly greased gratin dish and make 4 spaces for the eggs. Break the eggs into the spaces, then sprinkle the grated cheese on the top and bake the dish in the oven for 10–12 minutes until the eggs have set. Serve immediately.

OMELETTES

The omelette is a most versatile dish. It can be served at breakfast, lunch, or as a light main course. If you can, try to keep a special pan just for omelettes. A new pan should be seasoned first. To do this, pour oil into the pan to cover the base and come a little way up the sides. Warm this slowly, turning the pan gently so that the oil coats the sides. When both the pan and the oil are hot, remove from the heat and allow to cool. Do this once more using the same oil and then let the oil stand in the pan overnight. Next day warm the pan and oil again, pour off the oil and then wipe the pan dry. It will now be ready for cooking omelettes. Avoid washing the omelette pan after use. Instead wipe it clean with kitchen paper or a clean cloth.

SPANISH OMELETTE

A Spanish Omelette is also known as a tortilla and is served flat (i.e. it is not folded over in the pan). When the omelette is golden brown underneath, it can be turned with a spatula or the top cooked under the grill. The various regions of Spain have different versions of this recipe with potatoes as one of the most common ingredients. Tomatoes or other vegetables may also be added. I prefer to parboil potatoes first, as this means less oil is then needed to brown them in the pan. Serve this with green vegetables, or Ratatouille (page 177) for a light evening meal.

Serves 2
2 potatoes
1 onion, peeled and finely chopped
2 tablespoons oil
4 eggs
salt and freshly ground black pepper

Scrub the potatoes and chop them roughly, then parboil them in water for about 15 minutes. Heat the oil and gently fry the onion and potatoes until they are soft. Beat the eggs thoroughly in a small bowl and pour them over the potato and onion. Allow the eggs to set and the omelette to brown underneath, then either turn it over gently with a spatula or put the frying-pan under the grill to cook the top. Slide the omelette on to a warm serving plate and serve immediately.

FRENCH OMELETTE

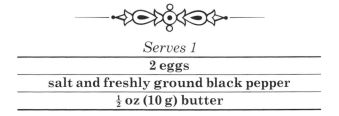

Serves 1
2 eggs
salt and freshly ground black pepper
$\frac{1}{2}$ oz (10 g) butter

Break the eggs into a cool dish and season well with salt and freshly ground black pepper. Whisk them thoroughly with a fork, remembering that one well beaten egg is worth two not so well beaten. Heat the pan, drop in the piece of butter and, as it foams, pour in the beaten egg. Shake the pan and as the egg begins to set, break it up lightly with a fork. Lift the cooked edges of the omelette and allow any uncooked mixture to flow under the cooked parts. When the bottom is browned, fold the omelette in half and tip it onto a warm serving plate.

81

OMELETTE FINES HERBES

Serves 1

2 eggs
salt and freshly ground black pepper
1 tablespoon mixed parsley, tarragon and chives, finely chopped
½ oz (10 g) butter

Break the eggs into a bowl, beat them thoroughly and season well. Then mix in half the chopped herbs. Heat the pan and drop in the butter, and, as it foams, pour in the beaten egg. Shake the pan and as the egg begins to set, break it up lightly with a fork. Sprinkle over the remaining herbs. Then start to lift the cooked edges of the omelette and let any uncooked mixture flow under the cooked parts. When the bottom has browned, fold the omelette in half and serve immediately.

TOMATO OMELETTE

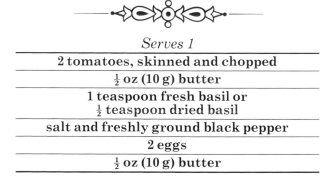

Serves 1

2 tomatoes, skinned and chopped
½ oz (10 g) butter
1 teaspoon fresh basil or ½ teaspoon dried basil
salt and freshly ground black pepper
2 eggs
½ oz (10 g) butter

Fry the tomatoes in the melted butter in a small pan for 2 or 3 minutes, then remove from the heat and mix in the basil and plenty of seasoning. Then make the omelette following the instructions in the previous recipe. When the eggs begin to set in the pan, add the tomatoes. When the bottom of the omelette has browned, fold in half and serve immediately.

PANCAKES

Wholewheat Pancakes 🐝 Spinach Wholewheat Pancakes
Tomato Wholewheat Pancakes 🐝 Buckwheat Pancakes
Dutch-style Cheese Pancakes
Mushroom and Watercress Pancake Filling
Chinese-style Vegetable Pancake Filling
Spiced Aubergine Pancake Filling 🐝 Ricotta Cheese and Herb Filling

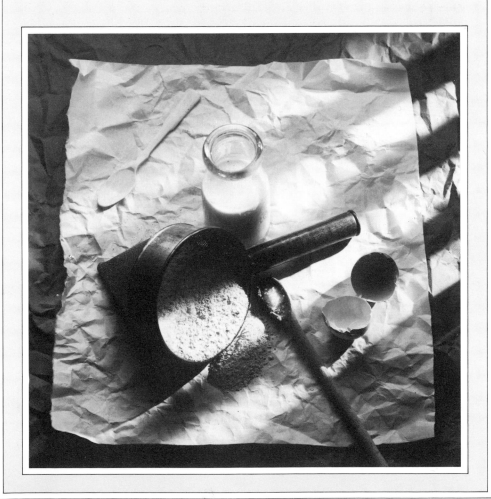

In Britain pancakes are mainly associated with Shrove Tuesday when, traditionally, they are served with lemon and sugar. But pancakes can be savoury too, making a splendid base for a meal at any time of the year. They are delicious made with wholewheat flour which, if you like, can be flavoured with spinach to make a delicately coloured variation. My favourite variety are buckwheat pancakes which have the distinctive dark colour of roasted buckwheat flour. These are a Breton speciality where savoury pancakes are called galettes and the sweet version is known as a crêpe. A liquidiser is ideal for mixing up pancake batter, but if you don't have one use the traditional method given.

Pancakes can be prepared well in advance as they keep in the refrigerator for 2–3 days, or in a freezer for longer if wrapped carefully in clingfilm or foil. They will thaw out in a short while and can then be filled, rolled and re-heated in the oven. When re-heating stuffed pancakes, they must be covered with either melted butter or a sauce and preferably cooked in a covered dish, otherwise they will become tough or over-crisp. Apart from the suggestions for fillings which I have given in this section the following recipes are also suitable: Stir-fry and Nitsuke Vegetables (pages 179–181) and Ratatouille (page 177).

Pancakes need not be served rolled up. They can be folded into four to form a fan shape which is popular in Holland, or they can be piled on top of one another with the filling sandwiched in between to form a 'gateau' which is cut into wedges to serve. This looks attractive as a party piece.

WHOLEWHEAT PANCAKES

Makes 10–12 pancakes

$\frac{3}{4}$ pint (400 ml) milk
1 large egg
pinch salt
1 teaspoon oil
6 oz (175 g) wholewheat flour

Liquidiser method
Put the milk, egg, salt and oil in the liquidiser and blend for 15–30 seconds. Then add the flour and blend for a further 30 seconds until the batter is smooth. I find the addition of oil makes the pancakes less likely to stick in the pan. If possible, let the batter stand for a while before you make the pancakes.

Traditional method
Put the flour and salt into a bowl. Beat together the egg, milk and oil, and pour this gradually into the flour and salt, stirring constantly, until a smooth batter is obtained.

To cook the pancakes
Heat a little oil in a frying-pan or skillet and when the oil is hot add 2 tablespoons of batter to the pan, quickly tipping it so the batter spreads out evenly into a circle. Let it cook for 2–3 minutes, then toss or flip over with a spatula and cook for a further minute or two.

Turn each pancake onto a cool surface if you wish to keep them for re-heating later, or place them on top of one another on a lightly oiled plate and keep warm in a moderately hot oven or under a low grill if you are going to fill them and eat them straight away.

SPINACH WHOLEWHEAT PANCAKES

These colourful pancakes make a change from plain wholewheat ones and are delicious served with a Ricotta Cheese and Herb Filling (page 92).

Makes 8–10 pancakes
4 oz (110 g) spinach
enough milk to make $\frac{1}{2}$ pint (275 ml) purée
1 egg
1 teaspoon oil
pinch of salt
3 oz (75 g) wholewheat flour

Wash the spinach several times in fresh changes of water, then shake off as much excess water as possible. Put the leaves into a heavy-based pan and cook for 6–8 minutes. Then purée in a liquidiser or press through a sieve, adding a little water. Allow to cool. Make the purée up to $\frac{1}{2}$ pint (275 ml) with the milk and then put this with the egg, oil and salt into the liquidiser and blend thoroughly for 30 seconds. Add the flour and blend again for another 30 seconds. Let the batter stand for a while before you cook the pancakes, following the instructions given in the previous recipe.

TOMATO WHOLEWHEAT PANCAKES

These are another version of wholewheat pancakes and they are delicious stuffed with the Spiced Aubergine Filling (page 91) or Ratatouille (page177).

Makes 8–10 pancakes
$\frac{1}{4}$ pint (150 ml) milk
$\frac{1}{4}$ pint (150 ml) tomato juice
1 egg
pinch salt
1 teaspoon oil
4 oz (110 g) wholewheat flour

Put the milk, tomato juice, egg, salt and oil into a liquidiser and blend thoroughly for 15–30 seconds. Then add the wholewheat flour and liquidise again for 15–30 seconds. Let the batter stand a little before cooking as described in the Wholewheat Pancake recipe (page 84).

BUCKWHEAT PANCAKES

If you've never tried using buckwheat flour before, you'll find it has an attractive speckled look and a distinctive flavour. It can easily be obtained in health food stores.

Makes about 8 pancakes
½ pint (275 ml) milk
1 egg
pinch salt
1 teaspoon oil
2 oz (50 g) wholewheat flour
2 oz (50 g) buckwheat flour

Put the milk, egg, salt and oil into a liquidiser and blend thoroughly for 15–30 seconds. Then add both flours and liquidise again for 15–30 seconds. If possible, let the batter stand before cooking as described in the basic Wholewheat Pancake recipe (page 84).

DUTCH-STYLE CHEESE PANCAKES

In this Dutch recipe, cheese is used in the batter, and the pancakes are stuffed with a light spinach filling. Serve them as a supper dish accompanied by Classic Tomato Salad (page 186).

Serves 4
For the pancake batter:
½ pint (275 ml) milk
1 egg
pinch salt
1 teaspoon oil
4 oz (110 g) wholewheat flour
3 oz (75 g) grated Gouda cheese

For the filling:
2 oz (50 g) butter
1½ oz (40 g) flour
¾ pint (400 ml) warm milk
12 oz (350 g) spinach
salt, freshly ground black pepper and nutmeg to taste

For the topping:
4 oz (110 g) grated Gouda cheese

First make the pancake batter. Put the milk, egg, salt and oil into a liquidiser and blend the mixture for 15–30 seconds. Then add the flour and cheese and blend again for 30 seconds. Let this batter stand for a while before making the pancakes. If you haven't got a liquidiser put the flour and salt in a bowl. Beat together the milk, egg and oil. Pour this into the flour and beat until you have a smooth batter. Then stir in the grated cheese.

Meanwhile prepare the filling. Melt the butter gently in a saucepan, stir in the flour and cook this roux for 3 minutes. Then pour on the warm milk, stir constantly and bring the sauce to the boil. Cook gently for 3–5 minutes.

Wash the spinach in several changes of water and cook it gently without water for 6–8 minutes in a covered, heavy-bottomed pan. When it is cooked, drain away any excess liquid and chop the cooked spinach into the white sauce. Remove the pan from the heat and season the sauce to taste. Then make the pancakes and keep them warm under the grill or in a moderate oven. When you have made 8, fill each one with about a tablespoon of filling. Roll them up and put them seam-side down into a lightly greased, shallow gratin dish and cover them with grated cheese. Heat these for 10 minutes in a very hot oven or put them under the grill until the cheese has melted. Serve immediately.

MUSHROOM AND WATERCRESS PANCAKE FILLING

Use this filling with either Buckwheat or Wholewheat Pancakes. The peppery flavour of watercress and the rich taste of mushrooms make a delicious and subtle combination. The best mushrooms to use are the flat or field mushrooms as they have such a good flavour. A tomato salad or lightly steamed green vegetable with some sour cream makes this a perfect meal.

Fills 6 pancakes

1 lb (450 g) mushrooms, wiped and very finely chopped
3 tablespoons spring onions, finely chopped
1 oz (25 g) butter
1 small bunch watercress, very finely chopped
salt and freshly ground black pepper
½ pint (275 ml) mixed soured cream and yoghurt or 1 recipe Tofu Dressing (page 205)

Melt the butter in a large saucepan and cook the onions for a few minutes. Add the very finely chopped mushrooms and cook for 10 minutes in an uncovered pan, stirring occasionally. (Quite a lot of liquid will be drawn out as they cook.) Remove the pan from the heat and strain the mixture reserving the juice for basting the pancakes. Put the cooked mushrooms and onions into a clean bowl and mix in the watercress. Season to taste. Use about a tablespoon of this mixture to fill each pancake, then put them into an ovenproof dish. Moisten the pancakes with a little of the mushroom liquid and re-heat in a moderate oven for about 10–15 minutes. Serve with the soured cream and yoghurt mixture of Tofu Dressing.

CHINESE-STYLE
VEGETABLE PANCAKE FILLING

This is a quick stir-fry filling for pancakes which is flavoured in the traditional oriental style with soy sauce and ginger. Stir-frying keeps vegetables crisp as they cook very quickly in just a few minutes over a high heat. Bean sprouts and spring onions are ideal for this as they are so crunchy and the bright colour of mange-tout looks perfect with the other vegetables.

Fills 4 pancakes

3 large spring onions, cleaned and finely chopped
3 oz (75 g) mange-tout, cleaned and sliced diagonally
4 oz (110 g) bean sprouts, rinsed
3 oz (75 g) mushrooms, wiped and sliced
1 tablespoon oil
$\frac{1}{4}$–$\frac{1}{2}$ teaspoon fresh root ginger, grated
1 teaspoon cornflour
1 teaspoon soy sauce

First prepare all the vegetables. Next heat the oil in a large frying-pan or wok and fry the grated root ginger. After 1 minute, when the oil is really hot, add the vegetables, turning them quickly in the frying-pan over a high heat for 3 minutes. Then sprinkle over the cornflour and soy sauce and cook the mixture for a further 3 minutes. Spoon the filling into the pancakes, roll them up and serve them straight away.

SPICED AUBERGINE PANCAKE FILLING

This filling is particularly delicious with Buckwheat Pancakes. It is quick to prepare and the sauté of aubergines and leeks makes a colourful combination highlighted by the spicy flavour of ginger and cayenne. This only needs the addition of sour cream to make a delicious light meal, served with a mixed green salad.

Fills 8 pancakes
3–4 tablespoons oil
1 lb (450 g) aubergines, washed and diced
$\frac{1}{2}$ teaspoon root ginger, freshly grated
1 clove garlic, crushed
$\frac{1}{4}$–$\frac{1}{2}$ teaspoon cayenne pepper
1 medium leek, cleaned and sliced
3 fl oz (75 ml) vegetable stock
1 teaspoon sugar
Garnish:
1 tablespoon chopped chives
$\frac{1}{4}$ pint (150 ml) soured cream
2–3 tablespoons yoghurt or single cream

Heat the oil and sauté the aubergines over a high heat for 3–4 minutes. Then remove from the pan using a slotted spoon. Re-heat the oil and add the ginger, garlic, cayenne pepper and sliced leek, and sauté this mixture briskly for about 30 seconds. Next pour in the stock and sugar and mix well. Return the aubergine cubes to the pan and cook the whole mixture for another minute. Spoon into the prepared pancakes and roll them up. Mix the soured cream with the yoghurt or cream and pour this over the pancakes. Sprinkle with chives. Serve straight away.

RICOTTA CHEESE AND HERB FILLING

This light filling is made with ricotta cheese which is a soft white Italian cheese. It is made from the whey of other cheeses and has a mild flavour that is suitable for sweet or savoury dishes. I have to order it from a local delicatessen but it is often obtainable in supermarkets. If you can't get it, a mixture of cream and curd cheese is a good alternative. Tomato Sauce (page 154) goes well with pancakes stuffed with this filling.

Fills 8 pancakes
1 bunch watercress
2–3 spring onions
2 tablespoons fresh parsley
$\frac{1}{2}$ lb (225 g) ricotta cheese
2 eggs
1–2 tablespoons Parmesan cheese, grated

Pre-heat the oven to gas mark 4, 350°F (180°C).

Wash and finely chop the watercress, spring onions and parsley. Beat these into the ricotta cheese until the ingredients are well blended. Mix in the eggs and Parmesan cheese. Fill each pancake with about 1–1$\frac{1}{2}$ tablespoons of filling, roll them up and place them, seam-side down, in a lightly greased, ovenproof dish. Brush them with a little oil, cover the dish with foil or a lid and bake them for 15–20 minutes. Serve hot accompanied by a sauce.

PASTA

Spaghetti with Mushroom and Garlic Sauce 🍍 Spaghetti Provençale
Spaghetti with Green Vegetables in Cheese Sauce 🍍 Pasta Parmigiana
Macaroni Cheese 🍍 Vegetable Lasagne with Cream Sauce
Spinach and Mushroom Lasagne

Two of the major advantages of wholewheat pasta are firstly that it can be kept in the store cupboard until needed and secondly, its versatility. Nowadays you can buy many varieties of wholewheat pasta which are easy and quick to cook and they are actually less likely to stick together than white pasta. For the simplest of meals serve pasta, freshly cooked, tossed in butter and garnished with cheese and parsley. Pasta such as spaghetti, tagliatelle or macaroni can be topped with a variety of sauces. Two suggested here are Mushroom and Garlic Sauce and a Provençale Sauce, but don't forget to look in the Sauces chapter (page 149) for other suggestions as most of the hot sauces there are also delicious served with pasta.

There are some more elaborate pasta dishes which can be prepared in advance and cooked in the oven, such as the classic Italian dish, Lasagne. I've included two versions of this which are always a success for both family meals and entertaining, and also an old favourite, Macaroni Cheese.

When cooking pasta use plenty of boiling salted water and a little oil to help keep the pasta separated. Most types of pasta cook in about 8–10 minutes. To see if it is done taste a piece — it should be *al dente* as the Italians say, soft but still with a 'bite' to it.

SPAGHETTI WITH MUSHROOM AND GARLIC SAUCE

Spaghetti can be served with any one of many different sauces for a quick and tasty meal. In addition to this one there are several other suitable sauces to choose from in the chapter on Sauces particularly Tomato Sauce (page 154). The vegetable casseroles such as the Basque Ratatouille (page 58) and Italian Fennel Casserole (page 64) are also good served with spaghetti.

Serves 4
For the sauce:
4 tablespoons olive oil
1½ lb (700 g) fresh tomatoes, skinned and sliced or 1 × 28 oz (800 g) tin of tomatoes
1 level teaspoon sugar
1 level teaspoon salt
1 bay leaf
12 oz (350 g) button mushrooms, wiped and thinly sliced
2–3 cloves garlic, crushed
2 teaspoons fresh marjoram or 1 teaspoon dried marjoram
freshly ground black pepper
12 oz (350 g) spaghetti
salt

Heat 2 tablespoons of the oil in a heavy-bottomed saucepan and add the tomatoes, salt, sugar and bay leaf. Cook slowly for 30 minutes in a covered pan. If you like a smooth texture you can liquidise the mixture at this stage. Then add the finely sliced mushrooms, crushed cloves of garlic, remaining olive oil and dried marjoram (if using). Add freshly ground black pepper and salt to taste. Simmer the mushrooms in the sauce until they are tender, which takes about 15–20 minutes, stirring occasionally. If you are using fresh marjoram, add it now.

Meanwhile prepare the spaghetti. Cook in plenty of boiling salted water for 8–10 minutes, then drain it and put into a warm serving dish. Pour on the hot sauce and serve immediately.

SPAGHETTI PROVENÇALE

This is a rich vegetable sauce for spaghetti which makes a very quick supper dish. It could be made a little more substantial by sprinkling cheese or buttered breadcrumbs on top and browning it under the grill. Mixed Green Salad (page 184) makes a good accompaniment.

Serves 4–6
For the sauce:
2 tablespoons oil
1 large onion, peeled and finely chopped
1 lb (450 g) courgettes, washed and diced
1 lb (450 g) mushrooms, washed and chopped
2 red or green peppers, de-seeded and diced
4 tablespoons tomato purée
1 pint (570 ml) stock or water
1 teaspoon dried oregano
1 teaspoon dried marjoram
salt and freshly ground black pepper
12 oz (350 g) spaghetti
salt
2 oz (50 g) Parmesan cheese

Heat the oil in a large pan and fry the onions gently for a few minutes. Prepare all the vegetables, add them to the pan and fry for a few minutes. (This process helps to seal in the flavours.) Add the tomato purée, stock, and herbs. Season well and cook for 20 minutes with the pan covered, stirring occasionally.

Meanwhile cook the pasta in plenty of boiling, salted water for 10 to 12 minutes until tender. Drain and put into a hot serving dish, top with the sauce and serve immediately, garnished with Parmesan cheese.

SPAGHETTI WITH GREEN VEGETABLES IN CHEESE SAUCE

This is a good dish to serve in the summer when the ingredients are plentiful and fresh. It is important to steam (rather than boil) the vegetables as this keeps them crisp and colourful.

Serves 4
For the sauce:
1 oz (25 g) butter
1 dessertspoon flour
½ pint (275 ml) warm milk
3 oz (75 g) Parmesan cheese, grated
2 tablespoons fresh parsley, finely chopped
1 small cauliflower, washed and broken into florets
8 oz (225 g) courgettes, washed and diced
4 oz (110 g) green beans, trimmed and cut into 1 in (2·5 cm) pieces
4 oz (110 g) peas, fresh or, if frozen, defrosted
juice of ½ lemon
1 oz (25 g) butter
salt and freshly ground black pepper
12 oz (350 g) spaghetti
salt

First prepare the sauce. Melt the butter in a small pan, add the flour, cook the roux for a few minutes. Then pour on the warm milk and, stirring constantly, bring it to the boil. Let it simmer over a gentle heat for 5 minutes. Then add half the Parmesan cheese and parsley.

Meanwhile prepare all the vegetables and steam them, either in a steamer or in a covered colander set over a pot of boiling water. Start with the cauliflower and after 5 minutes add the courgettes, beans and peas. When the vegetables are just tender, remove them from the heat and toss them in a large dish with the lemon juice, butter, salt and freshly ground black pepper.

Cook the spaghetti in plenty of boiling salted water for 8–10 minutes, then drain it and put it into a warm serving dish. Pile the vegetables on top of the cooked spaghetti and then sprinkle over the rest of the Parmesan cheese. Serve straight away and hand the sauce round separately.

PASTA PARMIGIANA

Though simple and quick to make, the use of cream in this dish makes it a deliciously rich one. If you prefer, substitute the healthier alternative of natural yoghurt for the cream. Serve on its own for a quick lunch or with green beans and grilled tomatoes for a light evening meal.

Serves 4
12 oz (350 g) pasta shells or spirals (try to get a wholewheat variety)
$\frac{1}{2}$ teaspoon salt
1 teaspoon oil
1 lb (450 g) mushrooms, wiped and chopped
1 green pepper, de-seeded and diced
1 red pepper, de-seeded and diced
2 tablespoons oil, preferably olive
juice of 1 lemon
$\frac{1}{4}$ pint (150 ml) single cream
salt and freshly ground black pepper
2 oz (50 g) Parmesan cheese, grated

Bring a large pan of water to the boil. Add the pasta shells, salt and oil and cook for 12–15 minutes until the pasta is tender. Meanwhile chop the vegetables into small, bite-size pieces. Heat the oil in a frying-pan, add the vegetables and cook quickly for 5–7 minutes, turning them frequently so that they don't brown.

Add the cooked, drained pasta, lemon juice, cream, salt and freshly ground black pepper. Stir well, then quickly pour this mixture into a gratin dish. Cover it with a thick layer of grated Parmesan and grill until the cheese is golden brown. Serve immediately.

MACARONI CHEESE

The first mention of Macaroni Cheese being eaten in England was in 1720 and it is hardly surprising that it is still popular today as it is both wholesome and tasty. It can be adapted very easily to suit wholewheat pasta, and wholewheat flour can be used for the sauce. As this combination produces a darker-coloured dish than the traditional one made with refined ingredients, I like to add extra colour by using plenty of chopped parsley. I also sprinkle over a cheese topping and grill this before serving the dish. This can be served with salad or steamed green vegetables for lunch or a light supper.

Serves 4
1 pint (570 ml) milk infused with ½ onion (peeled), 6 whole black peppercorns, 2 bay leaves, 1 teaspoon thyme and ½ teaspoon grated nutmeg
2 oz (50 g) butter
1 oz (25 g) flour
salt and freshly ground black pepper
6 oz (175 g) wholewheat macaroni
6 oz (175 g) grated Cheddar cheese
1 tablespoon freshly chopped parsley

First infuse the milk by bringing it just to the boil with the onion, spices and herbs. Remove the pan from the heat, cover it and allow the milk to stand for 10–15 minutes, then strain it. Meanwhile melt the butter over a gentle heat in a clean saucepan. Add the flour and cook this roux for 2–3 minutes. Pour over the infused milk, stirring all the time and bring the sauce gradually to the boil. Season well and then allow the sauce to simmer for 3–5 minutes, stirring occasionally.

Meanwhile cook the macaroni in plenty of boiling water for 8–10 minutes. When it is just cooked, drain and put it into a warm serving dish. Quickly stir 4 oz (110 g) of the grated cheese and the chopped parsley into the white sauce, then pour this over the cooked macaroni. Cover with the remaining cheese and grill the dish for 5–7 minutes until the cheese is bubbling and golden. Serve straight away.

VEGETABLE LASAGNE WITH CREAM SAUCE

Layered lasagne dishes are easy to prepare. Both wholewheat and the green spinach lasagne are now available as is lasagne with crinkled edges, known as lasagne ricci or lasagne lisci, and these make interesting variations. For special occasions I make this rich vegetable filling and layer it with a cream sauce. Serve with Mixed Green Salad (page 184) or a steamed green vegetable for a delicious and sustaining evening meal.

Serves 4–6

10–12 strips lasagne
2 onions, peeled and finely chopped
2 tablespoons oil
1 clove garlic, crushed
$\frac{3}{4}$ lb (350 g) mushrooms, wiped and sliced
$\frac{3}{4}$ lb (350 g) courgettes, washed and sliced
3 teaspoons dried oregano
1 lb (450 g) tomatoes, skinned and chopped
1 tablespoon tomato purée
salt and freshly ground black pepper

For the sauce:
1 oz (25 g) butter
1 dessertspoon flour
$\frac{1}{2}$ pint (275 ml) milk or single cream
2–4 tablespoons double cream (optional)
$1\frac{1}{2}$–2 oz (40–50 g) Parmesan cheese, grated

Pre-heat the oven to gas mark 4, 350°F (180°C).

First cook the lasagne as described on page 94. Then drain and rinse in cold water.

Gently fry the finely chopped onion in the oil for a few minutes and add the garlic. Then add the sliced mushrooms and courgettes and fry these for a few minutes to seal in the flavour. Add the oregano, tomatoes and tomato purée. Cover the pan and cook for 10–15 minutes so that the flavours have a chance to blend. Then season to taste.

Meanwhile prepare the sauce. Melt the butter in a small saucepan and stir in the flour. Cook the roux for 2–3 minutes, then pour over the milk. Bring it to the boil, stirring constantly and cook for

5 minutes over a gentle heat. Then add the cream and cook gently for another minute.

Lightly grease a 4 pint (2·3 litre) ovenproof dish and put in a layer of vegetable sauce. Cover with lasagne and then a layer of cream sauce. Repeat these layers ending with a layer of the cream sauce. Cover with grated cheese and bake for 35–40 minutes when the cheese should be bubbling and golden. Serve immediately.

SPINACH AND MUSHROOM LASAGNE

When making lasagne I find it easier to cook the strips of pasta in a roasting tin set on top of the cooker. Fill the tin with a couple of inches of water and add a little oil and salt. This way the blades of the lasagne can be placed in flat and they cook more quickly and are less likely to stick together. If you are preparing the pasta in advance, rinse the pieces in cold water immediately they are cooked. This will stop them from cooking any further and also prevents them becoming sticky.

Serves 4

8 strips lasagne (preferably wholewheat)
1¾ lb (800 g) spinach
1 teaspoon butter
1 teaspoon dried marjoram
12 oz (350 g) ricotta cheese or a mixture of curd and cream cheese
salt and freshly ground black pepper

For the sauce:
6 oz (175 g) mushrooms, wiped and sliced
1 oz (25 g) butter
¼ pint (150 ml) vegetable stock
1 teaspoon soy sauce
3 oz (75 g) Cheddar or Parmesan cheese, grated

Pre-heat the oven to gas mark 6, 400°F (200°C).

Cook the lasagne in plenty of boiling water for 8–10 minutes. Then drain and rinse in cold water.

Prepare the spinach by washing it in several changes of water. Put in a heavy-bottomed pan and cook gently without adding any water for 6–8 minutes. When it is cooked, strain off any excess water and chop finely. Return the spinach to the saucepan and season well. Put the pan on a gentle heat and add the butter and marjoram. Stir, then take the pan off the heat. When the spinach has cooled mix in the ricotta cheese or a mixture of curd and cream cheese. Season well.

Now prepare the sauce. Sauté the sliced mushrooms in butter, then reduce the heat and cook for 10 minutes in a covered pan so that plenty of juice is extracted. Add the stock and simmer for another 5 minutes. Purée for a few seconds in a liquidiser or put through a sieve or mouli. Add the soy sauce and season to taste.

Lightly oil a square or rectangular 3 pint (1·75 litre) dish. Spoon in some of the spinach filling, cover with 2 or 3 pieces of lasagne and then a coating of mushroom sauce. Repeat these layers ending with the mushroom sauce. Sprinkle over the grated cheese and bake for 35–40 minutes until the cheese is bubbling and golden. Serve immediately.

PASTRY

Wholewheat Shortcrust Pastry ❦ French Onion Tarts ❦ Asparagus Flan
Cheese and Tomato Flan ❦ Mushroom Flan ❦ Winter Vegetable Pie
Spiced Lentil Flan ❦ Wholewheat Flaky Pastry ❦ Florentine Pasties
Sussex Mushroom Pasties ❦ Spiced Pasties

Wholewheat pastry has a distinctive nutty flavour and it always looks appetising since it has a rich, golden brown colour. My Shortcrust Pastry recipe is particularly simple to make, rolls out very easily and keeps well. It makes an excellent base for flans. I've included one flan recipe which will particularly appeal to vegans, the Spiced Lentil Flan, since it uses no dairy produce or eggs, and many different fillings can be made based on the one used in this dish using purées of split peas or vegetables. Shortcrust pastry can also be used for pies and I've included a particularly delicious Winter Vegetable Pie which makes a lovely family supper meal.

For more special occasions, try making richer pastries using wholewheat flour. With a little practice you can produce light, airy results. My recipe for Wholewheat Flaky Pastry is particularly good for making pasties or pie toppings. I use a quick, easy method in which all the fat is added at once.

WHOLEWHEAT SHORTCRUST PASTRY

The best advice I was ever given about making pastry was that its success was merely a matter of paying attention to details. Pastry is, after all, only made from basic food stuffs — flour, fat and water — but by taking care with the way in which they are combined you can produce exceptional results. Plain shortcrust is the easiest to make and the proportions — generally half fat to flour — are not difficult to remember. What makes the difference between passable and perfect pastry is attention to details and one of these is: think cool while you are making it; think hot while you are baking it. Here are some guidelines about the basic ingredients.

Flour: Wholewheat pastry has a nuttier flavour and softer texture from that made with white flour. You will also need to use more water than is the case with white flour (generally about double the quantity but it will vary from one brand of flour to another). There are both self-raising and plain wholewheat flours on the market and I find that self-raising flour, or plain flour with baking powder, gives the pastry a lighter texture and prevents the base of a quiche or flan from becoming soggy.

Fat: I like to use a combination of fats, preferably equal quantities of solid vegetable fat and butter as I find the butter provides a very good flavour and the solid vegetable fat has good shortening qualities. Soft margarines and slimming margarines contain some water and this can upset the balance of the pastry so avoid them. Oil makes the pastry very soft to handle and gives rather too short and crumbly a texture. However, adding just a little oil keeps the pastry crisp and means you don't have to add quite so much water which can make the dough tough. I prefer to have the fat at room temperature for easier rubbing in.

Water: Use cold water to mix the dough together and don't pour it all in at once as this makes it harder to judge the right amount of liquid needed. Sprinkle it evenly over the top of the mixture, adding enough so that the dough will hold together and form a smooth ball. Too much water can make the pastry hard and tough and it will shrink drastically in the oven. However a dough that is slightly wet is much easier to roll out.

Sugar: I add a small quantity of sugar to both my sweet and savoury pastry as I find the sugar increases elasticity and makes it easier to roll out. Dissolve the sugar in the water before adding it to the dough because undissolved sugar grains show up as brown spots on pastry.

Makes approximately 8 oz (225 g) pastry dough

4 oz (110 g) wholewheat flour and **1 teaspoon baking powder** ***or* 4 oz (110 g) wholewheat** **self-raising flour**
pinch of salt
2 oz (50 g) mixed fats (half butter and **half solid vegetable fat)**
1 teaspoon brown sugar
3–4 tablespoons cold water
1 tablespoon oil

Pre-heat the oven to gas mark 6, 400°F (200°C).

Mix the flour and baking powder with the salt in a large bowl. Then mix together the two fats on a plate and chop them into pea-size pieces. Add them to the flour, mixing in with a knife so that all the pieces are lightly coated before you begin rubbing in. The coating of flour protects the pieces of fat from the warmth of your hands and keeps the whole dough cooler. Then rub the fat into the flour by lifting up pieces of fat with some flour and rubbing it in well between

105

your finger tips. Don't rub in the mixture too deep inside the bowl but lift it up fairly high as this will help put air into the dough and keep the mixture cool.

Rub in the fat until the mixture looks like fine breadcrumbs. There should be no loose flour in the bowl. If you shake the bowl occasionally as you rub in, the larger lumps of fat will rise to the top and you will see when all the fat has been evenly rubbed in.

Dissolve the sugar in 3 tablespoons of cold water and stir in the oil. Sprinkle this mixture evenly over the dough and stir it in with a knife. Only add as much water as is necessary to draw the mixture together so that the dough comes cleanly away from the bowl and forms a ball.

Turn out onto a lightly floured board and knead gently for a few minutes until the surface of the dough is smooth. It is very important to let the pastry rest now for 15–20 minutes in a cool place because a relaxed pastry is less likely to shrink in the oven, and the contrast of a hot oven and cool pastry causes expansion in the air trapped in the dough which gives the pastry a light texture.

After the pastry has rested, roll it out to the required size, preferably on a marble pastry slab or work-top to keep it cool. Use only a little flour on your board and rolling pin as too much extra flour added at this point will only upset the balance of the dough. Roll firmly and evenly in one direction turning the pastry round when necessary. If the dough contains the right amount of liquid you should find it easy to roll it out very thinly. When it is the right size, lightly flour the pin again, wrap the pastry around it and lift it onto the flan dish or baking dish. Press it in firmly so that no air is trapped underneath. Prick it all over with a fork and it is ready for baking.

I think it best to bake a pastry case blind (i.e. empty) and then fill it as this gives a crisper base. A metal flan tin on a baking sheet will help conduct the heat more efficiently. After 5–7 minutes in a hot oven the pastry will have set and become crisp. It can now be filled as required. Even if you are serving your pie or flan cold, it is usually tastier if the finished dish is re-heated slightly before serving.

If you find your finished pastry hard or tough it is probably because you haven't rubbed in the fat properly or you have not used enough fat. It could also be that you added too much water or that your oven was not hot enough. A soft crumbly pastry means that you probably used too little water or too much fat. With flan recipes, if you find your bases turn out soggy, it is a good idea to sprinkle the base with something that will absorb the juices from the filling, e.g. ground nuts, breadcrumbs or semolina. (Do this before you fill the flan!) This is a particularly useful tip for fruit flans.

FRENCH ONION TARTS

This is a traditional filling for tarts which is made rich and moist by the succulent onions. When you're cooking the onions be sure to fry them very slowly so they retain a juicy quality. I like to make small tartlets rather than one large flan as I think there's something especially appetising about an individual serving. These tarts are delicious hot, warm or cold.

Makes 6 tarts
1½ quantities of Wholewheat Shortcrust Pastry (page 104)
1 lb (450 g) onions, peeled and finely chopped
1½ oz (40 g) butter or 3 tablespoons oil
½ teaspoon salt
¼ teaspoon brown sugar
1 teaspoon fresh tarragon or ½ teaspoon freshly ground nutmeg
salt and freshly ground black pepper
2 eggs
2 fl oz (50 ml) single cream or evaporated milk
3 oz (75 g) Cheddar cheese, grated

Pre-heat the oven to gas mark 6, 400°F (200°C).

Roll out the pastry to fill 6 individual tartlet tins 2½ inches (7 cm) in diameter (or an 11 inch (28 cm) flan tin). Press the pastry firmly into the cases and prick well. Then bake for 5 minutes so that the pastry sets.

Meanwhile fry the onions in the butter or oil, taking care not to colour them. During the frying, lightly sprinkle them with salt as this brings out the juices. Then stir in the brown sugar and tarragon. Remove from the heat and leave the mixture to cool.

In a separate bowl beat the eggs thoroughly and then mix in the cream and grated cheese. When the onion filling is cool season with extra salt and black pepper. Mix it into the cheese and egg mixture and spoon this filling into the pastry cases. Bake for 30–35 minutes until the pastry shells are cooked and the filling is firm. Serve hot, warm or cold.

ASPARAGUS FLAN

Asparagus not only looks glamorous but it tastes delicious combined with this creamy flan filling. The spears are an ideal shape for circular dishes as they can be attractively arranged like the spokes of a wheel. This flan could be served hot or cold with a variety of salads. (NB You need to have a steady hand when carrying flans with liquid fillings to the oven. You may find it easier to set the pastry case ready inside the oven and pour in the filling from a jug, thus avoiding spillage.)

Makes an 8–9 inch (20·5–23 cm) flan
1 quantity of Wholewheat Shortcrust Pastry (page 104)
1 oz (25 g) butter
1 large onion, peeled and very finely chopped
1 clove garlic, crushed
3 eggs
$\frac{1}{4}$ pint (150 ml) milk
2 tablespoons double cream
salt and freshly ground black pepper
1 × 10$\frac{1}{2}$ oz (300 g) tin of asparagus tips

Pre-heat the oven to gas mark 6, 400°F (200°C).

Roll out the pastry to fill an 8–9 inch (20–23 cm) flan ring. Press it into the dish firmly and then prick it all over with a fork. Bake in the pre-heated oven for 5–7 minutes until the pastry has set. Then let the case cool slightly.

Meanwhile melt the butter gently, add the finely chopped onion and crushed garlic and fry for about 10 minutes. Do not let the onion colour. Then in a mixing bowl beat the eggs thoroughly and add the milk and cream and season well. Stir in the fried onion and garlic and then pour half of this mixture into the prepared flan ring. Arrange the asparagus tips, pointed ends towards the centre, over the top of the filling. Then pour on the remaining filling.

Bake for 35–40 minutes or until the centre feels firm. Serve hot or cold.

CHEESE AND TOMATO FLAN

Flans and quiches are easy to prepare and are equally tasty hot or cold. When I serve them at buffet parties I use double and single cream to make the filling special, but for everyday meals I tend to use milk. There are several cheeses which are suitable, particularly Cheddar, Lancashire and Gouda, because of their good flavour and texture when cooked. You could serve this flan with contrasting salads and baked potatoes.

Makes an 8–9 inch (20·5–23 cm) flan

1 quantity of Wholewheat Shortcrust Pastry (page 104)
6 tomatoes
1 bunch spring onions
6 oz (175 g) grated cheese
3 eggs
$\frac{1}{4}$ pint (150 ml) single cream or milk
salt and freshly ground black pepper

Pre-heat the oven to gas mark 6, 400°F (200°C).

Roll out the pastry to fill an 8–9 inch (20–23 cm) flan ring. Press it into the dish firmly and prick all over with a fork. Then bake for 5–7 minutes until the pastry has set. Let the flan case cool slightly.

Meanwhile prepare the tomatoes. Scald and peel them and cut them into thin slices. Clean and finely chop the spring onions. Sprinkle half the grated cheese into the bottom of the prepared flan case and arrange the slices of tomato on the top, then sprinkle over the spring onions.

In a medium-sized mixing bowl beat the eggs thoroughly, then mix in the cream or milk and remaining cheese. Season well and pour this over the layer of tomatoes and onions. Bake for 35–40 minutes. Serve hot or cold.

MUSHROOM FLAN

I like to use tiny button mushrooms for this filling so that they can be left whole, which looks very attractive. If you can only get large mushrooms, cut them into neat pieces. I serve this flan with a choice of salads.

Makes an 8–9 inch (20·5–23 cm) flan
1 quantity of Wholewheat Shortcrust Pastry (page 104)
1½ oz (40 g) butter
12 oz (350 g) tiny button mushrooms, wiped and left whole
3 eggs
¼ pint (150 ml) milk
2 tablespoons double cream
salt and freshly ground black pepper
paprika

Pre-heat the oven to gas mark 6, 400° F (200° C).

Roll out the pastry to fit an 8–9 inch (20–23 cm) flan ring. Press the pastry into the case well, prick all over with a fork and bake for 5–7 minutes. Then allow the case to cool slightly.

Meanwhile prepare the filling. Melt the butter very gently in a frying-pan and sauté the whole button mushrooms for 5–7 minutes over a very gentle heat. In a medium-sized mixing bowl beat the eggs thoroughly, add the milk and cream and beat thoroughly again. When the mushrooms are just soft remove the pan from the heat and allow to cool slightly. Then add them to the egg and milk mixture. Season well and pour this filling into the pre-baked flan ring. Dust the top with a little paprika then bake in the middle of the oven for 35–40 minutes or until the centre feels firm to the touch. Serve hot or cold.

WINTER VEGETABLE PIE

There are all sorts of different combinations of vegetables you can use to make rich and colourful pies, but it is important to achieve the right mix between soft and fibrous vegetables so that you get a good texture. This pie is good served with Savoury Brown Sauce (page 151) or Tomato Sauce (page 154), roast potatoes and lightly steamed green vegetables.

Serves 8
double quantity of Wholewheat Shortcrust Pastry (page 104)
1 tablespoon oil
1 onion, peeled and chopped
2 carrots, scrubbed and finely chopped
1 lb (450 g) courgettes, washed and diced
4 oz (110 g) mushrooms, wiped and sliced
2 tomatoes, washed and chopped
1 teaspoon fresh thyme or ½ teaspoon dried thyme
1 teaspoon fresh marjoram or ½ teaspoon dried marjoram
2 tablespoons fresh parsley, finely chopped
2 tablespoons tomato purée
1 tablespoon soy sauce
salt and freshly ground black pepper
beaten egg and salt for glazing

Pre-heat the oven to gas mark 6, 400°F (200°C).

Heat the oil in a large saucepan and gently fry the onions. Then prepare all the vegetables and add them to the pan with the herbs. Mix everything together well, cover the pan and cook gently until the vegetables are just soft. This takes about 10–15 minutes. Add the tomato purée, soy sauce and season to taste. Let the mixture cool.

Meanwhile line a 9 inch (23 cm) dish with the pastry. Fill it with the mixture, packing it down fairly firmly. Cover with a pastry lid and brush with the egg glaze. Prick the pastry so that the steam can escape and bake the pie for 35 or 40 minutes or until the pastry is crisp. Serve hot or warm.

SPICED LENTIL FLAN

This is a tasty and colourful flan filling made without dairy products so it is especially useful for vegans who don't eat these and for those who wish to cut down their consumption of eggs and cheese. (The pastry should, of course, be made with solid vegetable fat.) The lentils and spices make a good base for the colourful topping of lightly steamed courgettes. I've suggested using tofu — a soya bean curd rather like cream — to spread over the top, but you could use yoghurt instead.

Makes a 9 inch (23 cm) flan
1 quantity Wholewheat Shortcrust Pastry (page 104)
½ lb (225 g) red lentils
1 onion, peeled and finely chopped
1 tablespoon oil
2 teaspoons turmeric
1 teaspoon paprika
½ teaspoon ground cumin
12 fl oz (330 ml) water
2 tablespoons tomato purée
2 teaspoons fresh, chopped basil or 1 teaspoon dried basil
1 lb (450 g) courgettes, washed and sliced
10½ oz (297 g) packet Silken Tofu (see page 205)
juice of ½ lemon
1 clove garlic, crushed

Pre-heat the oven to gas mark 6, 400°F (200°C).

Pick the lentils over for sticks and stones, then steep them in hot water. Meanwhile prepare the onions. Heat the oil in a frying-pan and fry the onions together with the spices for a few minutes. Drain the lentils and add them to the pan. Fry for a few minutes, then add the water. Bring to the boil, then cover and simmer for 15–20 minutes until the lentils are just soft. Check on the amount of liquid about 5 minutes before the end of cooking and, should you need to add some more, add only a little at a time as the purée for this flan needs to be fairly thick. Then beat in the tomato purée and basil and let the mixture cool. Meanwhile steam the courgettes in a steamer or in a covered colander set over a pan of boiling water. Mix the tofu, lemon juice and garlic together and beat thoroughly or blend in a liquidiser for a few seconds.

Next prepare the flan case. Roll out the pastry to fill a 9 inch (23 cm) flan dish. Press it firmly into the base and prick well, then bake for 5 minutes to set the pastry. Spread the lentil and tomato mixture over the base of the flan and cover that with neatly arranged slices of courgettes. Pour over the tofu topping. Bake the flan for 35–40 minutes or until the centre feels fairly firm and the tofu is a light, beige colour. Serve warm or cold.

WHOLEWHEAT FLAKY PASTRY

In this type of pastry the dough rises in layers or flakes formed by a special rolling and folding process which builds up layers of dough and fat. This pastry will never be quite as flaky as that made by the traditional method using white flour (the texture is more of a cross between a flaky and a rough puff pastry), but it produces a deliciously rich pastry which is much quicker to make. It still takes some time to prepare, however, not so much in the method itself but in the time needed to chill and rest the dough in between the mixing and rolling out. Resting is absolutely essential for relaxing the stretched gluten and firming up the softened fat so that you get a better structure.

A high oven temperature is needed for this pastry as too cool an oven will cause the fat to run out and destroy the flaky layers. Here are one or two guidelines about the basic ingredients.

Flour: plain wholewheat flour should be used in this recipe as the raising agents in self-raising wholewheat flour will break up the strands of gluten in the dough which are necessary for the flaky result.

Fat: The ratio of fat to flour with flaky pastry is higher than with shortcrust. A mixture of butter and fat is used in equal proportions so that you get a good flavour and a good shortening quality. There are several brands of solid vegetable fat available in supermarkets and health shops. They are made from 100% vegetable oils which are then hydrogenated to make them solid. Keep the fats very cold so that you can grate them into the flour.

Liquid: cold water is used with lemon juice added. The lemon juice makes the gluten more elastic and then the dough is easier to roll out.

Remember when making this pastry to work in as cool a place as possible.

Makes approximately 1 lb 4 oz (560 g) pastry dough

6 oz (175 g) mixed fats (half butter and half solid vegetable fat)
8 oz (225 g) plain wholewheat flour
pinch salt
¼ pint (150 ml) cold water
squeeze of lemon juice

Pre-heat the oven to gas mark 7, 425°F (220°C).

Put the fats in the freezing compartment of a refrigerator half an hour beforehand so that they are really cold. Mix the flour and salt in a large mixing bowl. Grate in the fats and mix them lightly into the flour with a knife. Then add the water and lemon juice. Use a fork or palette knife to mix the flour, fats and water into a rough dough. Cover the dough with a damp cloth or polythene bag. This will prevent a dry skin forming on the surface of the dough. Chill for about 30 minutes.

Next remove the dough from the damp cloth or polythene bag and roll it out to an oblong strip about 5 × 15 inches (13 × 28 cm). Mark this oblong into thirds. Fold the pastry by turning the bottom up over the centre and the top third down over both. Press the side edges together with a rolling pin and give the pastry a quarter-turn clockwise. This means the open ends are facing towards and away from you, and the pastry will roll out more evenly because you are not rolling against a fold. Roll the pastry out again and repeat the folding process. Fold and seal again. Put the dough into a polythene bag and refrigerate for 30 minutes.

Remove the dough from the bag, then roll the pastry out again remembering to start with the open ends towards and away from you. Give a final roll and the pastry is ready to use. It is important when cutting flaky pastry to free all the layers by cutting the edges cleanly with a sharp knife and don't brush the edges with egg glaze because this would seal them and prevent the layers from rising. Always put flaky pastry onto a baking tray rinsed with a little cold water as this will help prevent the base scorching in the oven.

FLORENTINE PASTIES

Cheese, spinach and tomatoes make a wonderful combination for these light savoury pasties which are delicious hot or cold. If you can't buy mozzarella cheese, a Dutch Edam cheese is just as tasty. I like to serve these pasties with Tomato Sauce (page 154).

Makes 10 small pasties
1 quantity of Flaky Pastry (page 113)
double quantity of Tomato Sauce (page 154)
1¼ lb (560 g) spinach
1 large onion, peeled and finely chopped
1 oz (25 g) butter
salt and freshly ground black pepper
beaten egg for glazing
4 oz (110 g) mozzarella, Edam or Lancashire cheese

Pre-heat the oven to gas mark 7, 425°F (220°C).

First prepare the Tomato Sauce. Then pick over the spinach for any wilted leaves and wash it 3 or 4 times in a large bowl, using fresh water each time. Shake off as much excess water as possible. Put the spinach into a heavy-bottomed pan and cook it, covered, for 6–8 minutes over a gentle heat. It is not necessary to add any extra water. When it is cooked, drain away any excess water and squeeze out as much moisture as possible. Then chop the spinach thoroughly.

Fry the finely chopped onion in the melted butter for 5 minutes, then mix this into the cooked spinach. Season and moisten the mixture with 4 tablespoons of the prepared Tomato Sauce.

Roll out the flaky pastry very thinly and cut it into circles 3–4 inches (7·5–10 cm) in diameter. Place about 1 tablespoon of filling on each circle, then cover this with a slice of cheese. Brush the edges of the circle with beaten egg, fold in half, and pinch the edges together. Chill for 30 minutes. Then put the pasties on a wet baking sheet to prevent the undersides from scorching in the high heat of the oven. Glaze them with beaten egg and pierce a little hole in the top of each one to allow the steam to escape. Bake for 15–17 minutes. Serve warm, coated with the remaining Tomato Sauce.

SUSSEX MUSHROOM PASTIES

These delicious pasties make a good lunch or supper dish served hot with green vegetables and Onion Sauce (page 153), or cold with a selection of salads.

Makes 8–10 small pasties
1 quantity of Wholewheat Flaky Pastry (page 113)
1 tablespoon oil
1 lb (450 g) onions, peeled and finely chopped
1 clove garlic, crushed
8 oz (225 g) mushrooms, wiped and sliced
2 teaspoons dried mixed herbs
$\frac{1}{4}$ teaspoon cayenne pepper
salt and freshly ground black pepper
2 hard-boiled eggs
beaten egg and salt for glazing

Pre-heat the oven to gas mark 7, 425°F (220°C).

Heat the oil and gently fry the finely chopped onion and garlic for 3–4 minutes. Add the mushrooms, herbs and cayenne pepper and cook these over a gentle heat in a covered pan for 10 minutes. Then remove the pan from the heat.

Shell the hard-boiled eggs and chop the whites coarsely. Mash the yolks into the mushroom mix. Then add the chopped whites. Season the mixture to taste and let it cool completely.

Roll out the flaky pastry and cut it into 8 circles the size of a saucer. Brush the edges of each round with beaten egg then spoon 1 or 2 tablespoons of filling onto each and seal them up. Brush the outsides with extra egg and pierce a hole in the top to allow the steam to escape. If you have time, put the pasties in the refrigerator for 30 minutes before cooking as this gives the pastry a chance to rest and the end result will be better. Then bake the pasties in the oven for 15 to 20 minutes. Serve hot or cold.

SPICED PASTIES

Many countries have their own version of little pasties from the spiced samosas in Indian cookery to pasteles in the Middle East to our own famous Cornish pasty. The Northampton cobbler was a whole meal in one pastry case with the vegetables and potatoes at one end and jam and custard at the other. I've often wondered if there was a pastry arrow indicating where you were supposed to begin!

Pasties can be filled with a variety of different vegetables and either spiced, or seasoned with herbs. I prefer them hot with a sauce or ketchup but of course they are ideal for packed lunches or picnics. This version is filled with a spiced vegetable mix which has a pulse and grain base. I like this combination because the grain gives a chewy texture while the pulses add substance and colour, but you can make it just with vegetables, remembering to adjust the quantities.

Makes 8 small pasties

1 quantity of Flaky Pastry (page 113)
2 oz (50 g) aduki beans or brown lentils
2 oz (50 g) long grain rice, wheat grain or pot barley
2 pints (1·1 litres) water for boiling
1 small onion, peeled and finely chopped
2 carrots, scrubbed and diced
4 oz (110 g) mushrooms, wiped and diced
1 tablespoon oil
1 teaspoon turmeric
$\frac{1}{2}$ teaspoon ginger
$\frac{1}{2}$ teaspoon ground cumin
1 clove garlic, crushed
1 tablespoon tomato purée
salt and freshly ground black pepper
3–4 tablespoons stock or water
beaten egg for glazing the pastry

Pre-heat the oven to gas mark 7, 425°F (220°C).

You can use any combination of the pulses and grains that I've suggested. First pick them over carefully for sticks and stones and wash them thoroughly under a running tap. Then bring the mixture of pulses and grains to the boil in fresh water, cover the pan and simmer until they are tender. If you are using rice and aduki beans, the rice will cook first. With brown lentils and barley, the lentils will cook first. However, with a pasty filling it doesn't matter if the pulse-grain mixture is over-cooked as its purpose is to provide substance. A slightly over-cooked mixture will also help hold the filling together. When the pulse-grain mixture is cooked, drain it and reserve the stock for moistening the vegetables. Then set it aside to cool.

Meanwhile prepare the vegetables. Heat the oil and gently fry the spices. Add the finely diced vegetables together with the cooked pulses and grains and cook these gently for 10–15 minutes, stirring occasionally, and adding a little water if necessary. Then add the tomato purée, seasonings and a little extra stock to moisten. Cook for a further 5–7 minutes, then remove from the heat and let this mixture cool thoroughly.

When it is cold, divide the pastry into 8. Roll out each piece into a round the size of a saucer. Spoon 2 or 3 tablespoons of the filling into the centre of each round. Brush the edges with beaten egg, then fold them together to make a seam across the top. Seal and pinch the edges together. This is the traditional shape for a Cornish pasty. Brush the pasty with beaten egg, then make a small hole in the top of the pasty so that the steam can escape. Bake in a hot oven for 15–20 minutes until the pastry is a lovely golden brown. Serve hot or place them on a cooling rack if you want to eat them cold.

Pulses

Red Dragon Pie 🌱 Chilli Bean Casserole 🌱 Spiced Chick Peas
Vegetable Moussaka 🌱 Lentil Croquettes with Parsley Sauce
Savoury Beans with Cream and Parsley

I have always felt that poor little beans could do with a good publicity agent to improve their image. Many cooks avoid using them, usually, it seems, because they have the impression that bean cookery is full of dos and don'ts or perhaps because the taste of beans on their own isn't very exciting. So in my role of self-appointed PRO for the bean, I am glad to tell you that they do fit in with today's life-style. They can be very easy and quick to cook and, as an integrated part of a colourful tasty meal, they are a wonderfully versatile food.

A pulse is the seed of a pod-bearing plant hence the term encompasses beans, peas and lentils.

Pulses are among the oldest crops cultivated by man. In fact they were once held in high esteem practically to the point of worship. They are a very good source of protein and are low in fats and high in fibre — all good ingredients for a healthy diet. As a cook, I've found them a great source of inspiration.

Bean cookery has developed tremendously in recent years. The range of pulses on the market is now much greater and there is a wide choice of herbs and spices which can be used to flavour them. Also, a wider choice of exotic vegetables is available which combine well with beans to make interesting meals. They have many uses, from soups to salads through to savouries, pâtés and purées. I have adapted many dishes from around the world which use pulses in the most exciting and flavoursome ways. If you dislike the flavour of beans or have trouble digesting them, there are a few tips at the end of this section to show you how to overcome these problems.

BEANS

Aduki beans
Aduki beans are small red beans, much prized by the Chinese for their goodness. They have a strong nutty flavour, make good vegetarian burgers and loaves, and are useful for pie fillings and stuffing vegetables. Cooking method: ideally soak overnight, drain and rinse, then boil for 40–45 minutes until tender.

Black-eyed beans
Black-eyed beans are small, cream-coloured beans the size of a haricot bean but with a black spot. They have an earthy flavour and are particularly suitable for soups and casseroles. Cooking method: soak overnight, drain, rinse and boil for 40–45 minutes.

Flageolet beans
These delicate pale green beans are rather like a small kidney bean with a subtle nutty flavour. They are one of the finest pulses as they are harvested when young and small. They are excellent for salads, pâtés or purées. Cooking method: soak overnight, drain, rinse and boil for 1–1¼ hours.

Haricot beans
Haricot beans are small, oval, cream-coloured beans best known in their traditional form as baked beans when cooked with treacle and tomatoes. They mainly come from America (where they are known as navy beans) and are useful for soups and stews. Cooking method: soak overnight, drain, rinse and boil for 1 hour.

Mung beans
These are tiny, round, bright green beans which when sprouted are known as bean sprouts. They have a sweet pea-like flavour and cook fairly quickly. Cooking method: soaking is unnecessary; just rinse and boil for 30–45 minutes.

Red kidney beans
These are medium-sized beans with a bright, distinctive colour; they come mainly from the United States and Canada and are traditionally served with hot spices and chilli dishes. They are delicious in casseroles and salads. Cooking method: soak overnight, drain, rinse and boil for 45–50 minutes.

Chick peas
Chick peas are pale gold in colour and nutty in flavour and appearance. They are also known as garbanzos. Popular in Middle Eastern cookery, they are delicious in salads or for making savouries, pâtés and dips. Cooking method: soak overnight, drain, rinse and boil for 1–2 hours or more.

LENTILS

Split lentils
Bright orange or yellow in colour, these disintegrate in cooking and are usually served as a purée flavoured with herbs and spices, or are used for soups or thickening a stew. Cooking method: soaking unnecessary; just rinse and boil for 15–20 minutes.

Whole lentils

The most common varieties of these are green or brown. The brown ones are earthy-flavoured and the green ones have a more delicate flavour. The large green lentils are also known as continental lentils. They do not disintegrate in cooking and are good for soups and salads. Cooking method: no soaking necessary; rinse and boil for 40–45 minutes.

CLEANING AND WASHING

All beans and lentils should be picked over for small pieces of grit, ungerminated seeds and little sticks. The worst culprits are red lentils, but at least they are cheap and the quickest to cook. I've also found that the larger continental lentils and chick peas often have quite a lot of stones in them. Picking them over isn't a long job if you spread a few handfuls at a time on a plate; you'll probably only find two or three little stones per pound.

After you have picked them over, put the beans in a sieve and wash them through. This is just to get rid of any surface dust or dirt. Lentils or split peas are then ready to cook. The larger beans, however, do need some soaking. There are two main methods for dealing with such pulses: the soaking method which is the more traditional one, and the quick cooking method which is obviously better for busy cooks.

SOAKING METHOD

Soak the beans for several hours in plenty of cold water, allowing at least 2 pints (1·1 litres) to 4–8 oz (110–225 g) of beans. This process helps the beans to swell so that the final cooking time is reduced, and also helps remove some of the agents which cause flatulence and indigestion. Drain the beans and wash them under a running tap. Bring them to the boil in plenty of fresh water. I like to use a lot of water as it is useful for stock, so I cover them by at least 3 inches (8 cm). A tablespoon of oil helps to prevent a scum forming particularly with soya beans, black-eyed beans and butter beans. If you do get a scum then just skim it off.

Fast-boil the beans for at least 10 minutes. This is because there are toxins on the outside skin of beans, most of which are destroyed by the soaking and cooking process. However, with some beans, particularly red kidney beans, the toxins will only be destroyed by at least 10 minutes of fast boiling. I think it's simpler to apply that rule to all beans. After fast-boiling the beans, turn the heat down to simmer, partially cover the pan and continue cooking them until they are soft.

Do not add salt to the cooking water as this toughens the outside skin of the pulses and means they will take longer to cook. Cooking times for different types of beans and peas can vary greatly either from batch to batch, or according to the country of origin or to the age of the crop. The longer you have had the beans the longer they will take to cook. Cooking time also depends on whether you need them to be soft enough to mash or just tender enough for a crunchy salad. The times given here are therefore only a rough guide. When the beans are cooked, drain off the liquid (keeping it for stock) and use as required.

QUICK COOKING METHOD

Wash the beans and bring them to the boil in plenty of fresh water. Boil them fast for 3–5 minutes. Turn off the heat and let the pulses soak in that water for one hour. Then drain off the liquid and re-boil the pulses in fresh water as described in the soaking method. The first quick boil and one hour of soaking are a substitute for the long overnight soak.

USING A PRESSURE COOKER

If you use a pressure cooker the cooking time is reduced by at least half, but do be careful not to put in too many beans at once. This is particularly important with beans which form a scum such as black-eyed beans or soya beans as the scum can block the safety vent. I use a pressure cooker when I want to have the beans soft enough for soups or purées. Where the appearance of the bean is important I think it's better to cook them in an ordinary pan as they are less likely to lose their shape. With the pressure cooker method you don't have to worry about fast boiling as obviously the beans are kept at a very high temperature throughout the cooking period.

FRYING IN OIL

The flavour of beans can be improved if they are gently fried in a little oil. After washing and soaking, drain the beans and use up to 1 tablespoon of oil per 8 oz (225 g) of beans. Heat the oil in the pan, then fry the beans for 2 to 3 minutes on a gentle heat adding a clove of garlic, spices or a chopped onion if you wish. Stir occasionally, then pour on the water and cook as usual. This makes the beans much more creamy, especially if you use olive oil, and is a method much used in South American and Mexican cookery. If you are calorie-conscious and don't want to use oil, you could flavour the water in which the beans are cooked with different vegetables or herbs such as onions, carrots or a bouquet garni. This will make the stock and the beans tastier.

COMBINING DIFFERENT VARIETIES

I like to mix together several different pulses in the same dish. If you decide to try this, however, don't cook red and white beans together or they will all end up pink! The red bean group includes red kidney beans, aduki beans and brown lentils and these could be cooked together satisfactorily. The brown lentils will of course be cooked quite a long time before the red kidney beans are ready. This is useful when you are making a mixed bean soup as some will cook to a purée, giving the soup thickness, and others will just become tender, giving the soup a nice texture.

STORING AND FREEZING COOKED PULSES

Bean liquid will keep for a few days and beans, well drained, for four to five days if stored in a covered container in the refrigerator. Beans will also freeze very well, either in their cooking liquid or well drained and stored in a plastic container. Just take out the container when needed and bang it firmly on a table top. The top layer of beans will shake loose and they can be used straight away.

DIGESTING PULSES

If you find beans indigestible add caraway, aniseed, fennel, or asafoetida to the cooking liquid. Half a teaspoon will be plenty for up to 8 oz (225 g) of beans. All these spices help the digestion or, as Culpeper puts it in his book *British Herbal* (1652) 'they ease the pain of windy colic'. Some pulses are more easily digested than others so if you are unfamiliar with them start with the lentil and split pea family, aduki beans and black-eyed beans.

RED DRAGON PIE

This makes a good supper dish. It is like shepherd's pie but is made with a rich bean and vegetable mixture topped with mashed potato. The Chinese call aduki beans 'red dragon' or 'red wonder' beans as they have found them to be so full of goodness. The cooking liquid from aduki beans is thought by some to be a tonic for the kidneys. Serve this pie with green vegetables and a tomato or mushroom sauce. Maybe you will have the power of the dragon after eating it!

Serves 4

4 oz (110 g) aduki beans
2 oz (50 g) wheat grain or rice
2 pints (1·1 litres) water for soaking
2 pints (1·1 litres) water for boiling
1 tablespoon of oil
1 onion, peeled and finely chopped
8 oz (225 g) carrots, scrubbed and diced
1–2 tablespoons soy sauce
2 tablespoons tomato purée
1 teaspoon mixed herbs
$\frac{1}{2}$ pint (275 ml) aduki bean stock
salt and freshly ground black pepper
1 lb (450 g) potatoes, peeled
1 oz (25 g) butter

Pre-heat the oven to gas mark 4, 350°F (180°C).

Wash the aduki beans and the wheat grain or rice and soak them overnight or steep them in boiling water for 1 hour. Drain and rinse, then bring them to the boil in fresh water and cook for 50 minutes or until the wheat grain or rice is fairly soft. Drain, reserving the stock.

Heat the oil in a saucepan and fry the onion for 5 minutes. Add the carrots and cook for 2–3 minutes. Then add the cooked beans and grains. Mix the soy sauce, tomato purée and herbs with the stock. Pour this over the bean and vegetable mixture. Bring to the boil and simmer for 20–30 minutes, so that the flavours are well blended. Season to taste. Add a little more liquid if necessary so that the final mixture is moist. Transfer into a greased 3 pint (1·5 litre) casserole.

Boil the potatoes until soft and mash them with butter. Season well. Spread the mashed potatoes over the beans and vegetables. Bake for 35–40 minutes until the potato is crisp and brown.

CHILLI BEAN CASSEROLE

This is definitely a dish for wintry days, of which we have many. The bulgar wheat swells up in the liquid during cooking and gives a lovely texture preventing the dish from being sloppy without making it too heavy. If you can't get bulgar wheat, use some uncooked rice or oat flakes to thicken the stew and give it texture. You can cook this dish on top of the cooker or in a moderate oven. It goes well with a crunchy salad and yoghurt or sour cream.

Serves 4

$\frac{1}{2}$ lb (225 g) uncooked red kidney beans
2 pints (1·1 litres) water for soaking
2 pints (1·1 litres) water for boiling
1 tablespoon olive oil
$\frac{1}{2}$ lb (225 g) onion, peeled and finely chopped
1 clove garlic, crushed
$\frac{1}{2}$ lb (225 g) mixed vegetables, scrubbed and chopped (e.g. celery, pepper, carrot)
$\frac{1}{2}$ teaspoon dried basil
$\frac{1}{2}$ teaspoon ground cumin
$\frac{1}{4}$ teaspoon cayenne pepper
$\frac{1}{4}$ teaspoon chilli powder
1 × 14 oz (400 g) tin of tomatoes, liquidised
2 tablespoons tomato purée
3 tablespoons red wine
2 oz (50 g) bulgar wheat
1–1$\frac{1}{2}$ pints (570–900 ml) stock (liquid reserved from cooking the beans)
juice of $\frac{1}{2}$ lemon
salt and freshly ground black pepper

Soak the beans overnight in water, drain and rinse well. Bring them to the boil in fresh water and boil fast for at least 10 minutes so that any toxins on the outside of the beans are destroyed. Then cover the pot and simmer for a further 35–40 minutes. If you find that the water tends to boil over, it helps to add a teaspoon of oil. When the beans are soft, drain and reserve the stock for use later.

Heat the oil in a large saucepan, gently fry the onions and garlic for a few minutes and then add the chopped vegetables, beans, basil and spices. Stir well and cook for 5 minutes as this helps seal in the flavour and some of the nutrients. Next add the tomatoes, tomato purée, red wine, bulgar wheat and 1 pint (570 ml) of stock. Bring the mixture to the boil, cover the pan and simmer for about 30 minutes. Add the lemon juice and seasonings and increase the stock level if you like your casseroles fairly liquid, then cook for a further 20–30 minutes. If you want to cook this dish in the oven, transfer the mixture, after bringing it to the boil, to a casserole and cover. It will take about 50–60 minutes at gas mark 4, 350°F (180°C). Don't forget to add the lemon juice and seasoning half-way through the cooking time. Serve hot.

SPICED CHICK PEAS

This is a warming, satisfying dish and can also be made with red kidney beans or haricot beans. Chick peas are a pale golden colour with a distinctive nutty flavour. They are certainly one of the most versatile beans as they can be used equally well in strong, spicy dishes or milder, creamier ones. I like to cook chick peas so that they stay crunchy to give the dish a better texture. Serve this with brown rice and a refreshing salad.

Serves 4–5

6 oz (175 g) chick peas
3 pints (1·75 litres) water for soaking
3 pints (1·75 litres) water for cooking
2 tablespoons oil
2 medium onions, peeled and finely chopped
½ teaspoon chilli powder
1 teaspoon ground coriander
1 teaspoon root ginger, freshly grated
1 teaspoon ground cumin
2 red or green peppers, de-seeded and finely chopped
4 tablespoons tomato purée
½ pint (275 ml) stock reserved from cooking the beans
lemon juice to taste
salt and freshly ground black pepper

Pick the chick peas over carefully for any stones or sticks, then soak them in water overnight or all day. After soaking, drain off the water and rinse them well under a running tap. Bring to the boil in fresh water and fast-boil for at least 10 minutes. Skim off any scum that forms on the surface. Lower the heat, partially cover the pan and cook the chick peas until they are tender. This can depend on the age of the chick peas and will take anything from 50 to 90 minutes. When they are cooked, drain off the cooking liquid and reserve ½ pint (275 ml) of it for stock.

Heat the oil in a large saucepan and gently fry the finely chopped onion together with the spices for 5–7 minutes. Then add the finely diced peppers and cooked chick peas. Dissolve the tomato purée in the stock and mix this into the vegetables. Cook for 10 minutes, then taste for seasoning and add a little lemon juice, salt and freshly ground black pepper. Serve immediately.

VEGETABLE MOUSSAKA

When I lived in the Sudan, aubergines were very much part of the staple diet, starting with aubergine jam for breakfast and finishing with aubergine stew at night. This dish is one of my favourite ways of eating them and is delicious served with steamed courgettes, broccoli and Tomato Sauce (page 154).

Serves 4
2 oz (50 g) green or brown lentils
1 pint (570 ml) water
4 tablespoons oil, preferably olive
1 onion, peeled and finely chopped
1 clove garlic, crushed
$\frac{1}{4}$ lb (110 g) mushrooms, wiped and chopped
2–3 tablespoons tomato purée
2 teaspoons dried oregano
1 teaspoon freshly grated nutmeg
salt and freshly ground black pepper
12 oz (350 g) or 2 medium aubergines, washed and sliced
2 potatoes, scrubbed, boiled and sliced
2 tomatoes, washed and thickly sliced

For the sauce:
$\frac{3}{4}$ oz (20 g) butter
1 tablespoon flour
8 fl oz (225 ml) milk
1 small egg
$\frac{1}{2}$ teaspoon mustard powder
salt and freshly ground black pepper
3 oz (75 g) grated Cheddar cheese

Pre-heat the oven to gas mark 4, 350°F (180°C).

Pick the lentils over for sticks and stones, wash them thoroughly, then bring to the boil in the water. Cover and simmer for 40–45 minutes or until they are soft. When cooked, drain and reserve the liquid for stock.

Heat 2 tablespoons of oil in a frying-pan and fry the onion and garlic gently so that they remain translucent. Then add the chopped mushrooms and cooked lentils and cook for a further few minutes, mixing well. Remove the vegetables from the pan using a slotted spoon so that as much oil as possible is left in the frying pan.

Put the vegetables into a bowl and mix in a little stock, 2–3 tablespoons of tomato purée and the oregano. Season well with nutmeg, salt and freshly ground black pepper. Then add 2 more tablespoons of oil to the frying-pan and fry the aubergine slices until soft, turning them over constantly. (You may need a little extra oil for this.) Put the slices onto a piece of kitchen paper to drain and let them cool.

Grease a 3 pint (1·75 litre) ovenproof dish and put in a layer of lentil and mushroom mixture, then a layer of aubergines, then of potato and tomato slices.

Next make the white sauce. Melt the butter in a small saucepan and stir in the flour. Cook the roux for 2–3 minutes. Pour on the milk and bring the sauce to the boil, stirring constantly. Simmer for 5 minutes and then allow to cool. Beat in the egg and season the sauce well with mustard, salt and freshly ground black pepper. Pour the sauce over the top of the casserole and sprinkle over the grated cheese. Bake for 40 minutes until the cheese is golden brown and bubbling. Serve piping hot.

LENTIL CROQUETTES WITH PARSLEY SAUCE

I like the combination of lentils and cheese in these croquettes which makes them both tasty and nutritious. As with most pulses a little sharpness added to the purée gives them a better flavour and here I've used a teaspoon of lemon juice. If you are in a hurry you can make the mixture up and use it straight away, but it is better to make it well in advance so that the flavours have a chance to blend. Also it is easier to handle this kind of mixture when it is cold. I've suggested a parsley sauce to go with this recipe but Tomato Sauce (page 154) would be just as good. I serve these croquettes with rice and green vegetables.

Serves 4

8 oz (225 g) red lentils
1 pint (570 ml) water
1 teaspoon oil
4 oz (110 g) Cheddar cheese, grated
2 tablespoons peanut butter
2 oz (50 g) fresh wholewheat breadcrumbs
2 teaspoons fresh parsley, finely chopped
a few drops of lemon juice
1 teaspoon yeast extract
salt and freshly ground black pepper

For coating:
1 beaten egg
3 oz (75 g) fresh wholewheat breadcrumbs

For the sauce:
$\frac{3}{4}$ pt (400 ml) White Sauce (page 152)
1 tablespoon fresh parsley, finely chopped

Pick the lentils over for stones and wash them thoroughly under a running tap. Bring them to the boil in the water and then add a teaspoon of oil as this will make the lentils softer and creamier and will also prevent the water from boiling over. Let the lentils simmer, covered, for about 20 minutes until they are soft. Then turn down the heat and beat them thoroughly to dry the purée out slightly and make it very smooth. It will thicken as it cools. Remove the pan from the heat and let the purée cool completely. Then mix in the other ingredients, seasoning to taste. Shape the mixture into 8 croquettes. Dip each croquette into the well beaten egg and coat it in bread-crumbs. Put them into the refrigerator for at least 30 minutes before you cook them.

Meanwhile prepare the sauce by making up $\frac{3}{4}$ pint (400 ml) of White Sauce and stirring into it a tablespoon of fresh parsley. Heat the sauce through slowly while you fry the croquettes in a small amount of oil. They take about 5–7 minutes on each side so that the outsides are nicely crisp and the mixture is cooked right through. Transfer to a warm serving dish, cover with sauce and serve straight away.

SAVOURY BEANS WITH CREAM AND PARSLEY

Creamy white haricot beans are the perfect colour to be teamed with bright green parsley for this recipe. The beans are tossed in butter and then cooked lightly in a cream sauce. It is delicious served either as a main course with a hot or cold rice dish and a fresh salad, or as a side vegetable with a savoury flan or vegetable casserole.

Serves 2–3 for a main meal, 4 for a side vegetable

½ lb (225 g) haricot beans
3 pints (1·75 litres) water for soaking
3 pints (1·75 litres) water for cooking
2 oz (50 g) butter
salt
¼ teaspoon cayenne pepper
1 egg yolk
2 tablespoons single cream
2 oz (50 g) grated Cheddar cheese
2 tablespoons fresh parsley, finely chopped
Garnish:
wedges of lemon

First prepare the beans by soaking them overnight or all day. Then drain off the water, rinse thoroughly and bring to the boil in a large saucepan of fresh water. Fast-boil the beans for 10 minutes, skimming off any scum that may form on the surface. Then turn the heat down, partially cover the pan and let the beans cook for a further 40 minutes until they are just soft. Drain away the excess water keeping it for stock or soup bases for other recipes.

Next melt the butter in a large saucepan, add the beans and season well with salt and a little cayenne pepper. Toss them in the butter for 2 or 3 minutes on a low heat. In a small bowl beat together the egg yolk and cream and then stir this mixture into the beans. Add the cheese and, when this has melted, the parsley. Transfer to a warm serving dish, garnish and serve immediately.

RICE and GRAINS

Plain Brown Rice 🐜 Fried Rice 🐜 Spiced Almond Risotto
Spiced Vegetable Pilau 🐜 Chinese-style Vegetables with Rice
Savoury Golden Rice Ring 🐜 Cashew Paella 🐜 Risotto Piedmontaise
Spiced Savoury Crumble 🐜 Tibetan Roast

As well as a wide variety of beans to choose from, there are also seven major grains we can eat. These are barley, maize or corn, millet, oats, rye and, most familiar of all, wheat and rice. Buckwheat is sometimes included as the eighth member of this group, though it is not strictly speaking a grain, but a seed.

Grains can be found in an amazing number of guises from bread to porridge oats, popcorn to barley wine. It is fascinating to think that the cultivation of grains changed the nature of our civilisation from that of a nomadic hunting existence to a largely sedentary, harvesting one, since once crops were planted a settled community was needed to farm them. Many cultures around the world have grown up around a particular grain, using it as their particular staple food. In the Far East, communities depend on rice and millet, in the Americas it is maize and in Europe wheat has been the principle grain for centuries. Rye is popular in Scandinavia and buckwheat in Russia where it is used to make a type of porridge called kasha. In Great Britain there are also regional specialities, such as Scottish oatcakes and Yorkshire frumenty, which is a soaked wheat-grain dish.

Grains have remained an important part of our diet because they are so versatile and relatively inexpensive. They are a good source of protein, and doctors and nutritionists also recommend them for their high fibre, high carbohydrate and low fat content.

Grains can be used in a variety of forms. They can be cooked whole, e.g. rice grain in risotto. They can be used in flake form, as in porridge oats, or when ground they are used in cakes, pastries and as thickening agents. You may be very familiar with a grain in one form but not use it at all in any other guise. We don't find it at all odd to use barley in soups but most of us wouldn't normally consider barley flour for bread-making. Of course not all grains are suitable for *every* type of cooking. Wheats are generally considered to be the best grains to use for bread because the high gluten content makes an elastic dough which can easily be expanded by yeast, whereas the creamy quality of oats makes them very suitable for breakfast cereals.

However, it is well worthwhile experimenting with different grains in recipes. For example, one success I have had is to cook small quantities of barley and wheat and add them to rice salad. This gives an attractive speckled look to the salad. It is also interesting to try out small quantities of different flours in bread-making.

TOASTING GRAINS

Grains are tastier if they are lightly fried or 'toasted' before they are cooked. This applies particularly to millet, buckwheat and barley. Use about 1 teaspoon of oil for 4–8 oz (110–225 g) of grains, heat the oil and then fry the grains. Millet and barley will turn a golden brown colour and buckwheat a dark, toasted colour. This only takes seconds but it will really bring out the flavour. Then pour on the boiling water and cook as usual.

Grains can be fried with spices, a technique particularly suitable for Indian rice dishes, and also the cooking liquid, which may be water or milk, can be flavoured with herbs and vegetables for extra taste.

TYPES OF GRAIN

A short description of each grain will introduce you to its particular qualities.

BARLEY

This is a pale round grain which is sold as either pot or pearl barley. It is mainly used for soups. Drinking barley water (which is an infusion of the grain) is said to be very good for the complexion.

Cooking method to use barley like rice: wash the barley. Heat a teaspoon of oil in a pan and lightly toast it. Then pour on hot water using 3–4 cups of water per cup of grain. Stir once. Cover the pan and cook for approximately 50–60 minutes, stirring occasionally, or until the grains have burst and are soft. You may need to add a little more water during cooking.

BUCKWHEAT

This isn't strictly speaking a grain, but a relation of the rhubarb family, in fact, though the dark angular seeds are used just like cereal grains. They are rich in vitamin B. When added to casseroles and hot-pots buckwheat helps make a richer, heartier dish. In Brittany speckled buckwheat flour is used to make a delicious, light, savoury pancake which is called a galette.

Cooking method to use buckwheat like rice: wash the buckwheat. Heat a teaspoon of oil in a pan and lightly toast it. Then pour on hot water using $2\frac{1}{2}$–3 cups of water per cup of grain. Bring to the boil, stir once and cover the pan. Cook for 20 minutes or until the grain is soft and chewy.

135

CORN OR MAIZE

Usually known in this country as corn and in the Americas as maize, corn is usually eaten in three forms – sweetcorn, popcorn, and maize flour or cornmeal. The colour of the grain is golden. It has a light, sweet flavour and the flour or meal makes delicious yellow custard, and golden bread and muffins. White cornflour is the starch of the grain which is used as a thickener for sauces, but it has little nutritional value.

MILLET

Millet is light and fluffy when cooked and is a good substitute for rice. It is extremely quick to cook and is easily digested. I think its best use is in pilaus or risottos because it combines so well with other vegetables. I've also found it makes a splendid change from rice in 'rice' pudding.

Cooking method to use millet like rice: wash the millet. Heat a teaspoon of oil in a pan and lightly toast it. Then pour on hot water using $2\frac{1}{2}$–3 cups of water per cup of millet. Bring to the boil, stir once and cover the pan. Cook for approximately 20 minutes until the water is absorbed and the millet grains are fluffy.

OATS

Oats have a delicious creamy flavour and combine well with nuts in savoury dishes as well as making delicious sweet and savoury biscuits, cakes and pancakes. Oatmeal can also be used as a thickener for soups and stews. Porridge oats, which are an important ingredient in muesli, are the quickest to cook. If you ever have a chance to buy whole oats – known as oat groats – do try them. They have a wonderful sweet flavour and make a wholesome porridge.

RICE

Rice is one of the most versatile grains and comes in several forms: brown or white, long-grain or short-grain.

After wholewheat bread, brown rice must be the next most familiar wholefood ingredient. I discovered very quickly how much I preferred its nutty flavour and firm texture to the rather bland, soft, white variety. Brown rice also contains more vitamin B, dietary fibre and minerals than white rice. Although it takes slightly longer to cook it is easier to use as the grains never stick together.

Brown rice can be substituted for white in virtually any recipe. If you haven't tried it before you might like to use half brown rice and half white rice at first, cooking them in separate pans and mixing them together before serving. This way you can accustom yourself more gradually to the extra nuttiness.

Long-grain rice is usually used for savoury dishes, but the short-grain can always be used instead, although it is better for making creamier dishes such as risottos. Brown rice also makes a good change from potato or pasta as an accompaniment to other dishes. You can serve it plain or make a number of very simple variations to complement whatever else is cooking. Brown rice keeps for up to six months in a cool dry place.

Finally, rice flour is a pale flour which when combined with wheat flour gives cakes a light, slightly crumbly texture.

PLAIN BROWN RICE

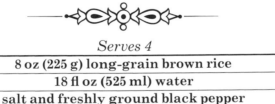

Serves 4

8 oz (225 g) long-grain brown rice
18 fl oz (525 ml) water
salt and freshly ground black pepper

First wash the rice thoroughly. Then bring the water to the boil and add the rice, stirring once. Cover the pan and cook gently for 25–30 minutes. All the water should have been absorbed and the rice will be cooked. It will have a slightly chewy texture as brown rice is never as soft as white rice. Season well and serve.

FRIED RICE

The simplest fried rice can be made by just adding a teaspoon of spice to the rice. Use turmeric to produce a golden colour and curry flavour, and paprika for a russet colour and a mild peppery flavour which makes a good accompaniment to vegetable casseroles.

Serves 4
8 oz (225 g) long-grain brown rice
2–3 tablespoons oil
1 onion, peeled and finely chopped
1 teaspoon turmeric or   **1 teaspoon paprika**

Cook the rice as described in the basic Plain Brown Rice recipe (page 137). Heat the oil in a frying-pan and fry the onion and spice gently for a few minutes. Then add the cooked rice and stir quickly as it heats through. Serve immediately.

RYE

Rye grain and rye flakes are dark in colour and have a strong tangy flavour; they are both used for the black breads which are so popular in Northern Europe. I think they are at their best in breads as the grains on their own are rather tough and chewy. Rye flour is low in gluten so it makes flatter loaves. Consequently, with the exception of pumpernickel, most rye loaves are made with a mixture of rye and wheat flour.

I think rye flour has a most interesting flavour and it is worth substituting 1–2 oz (25–50 g) of it for some of the wholewheat flour in bread to give the dough an entirely different flavour and texture.

WHEAT

Wheat is the staple grain in Britain and indeed in half the countries of the world. We use wheat flour to make bread, cakes, pastries, biscuits and puddings. Wheat is either hard or soft. Hard wheats, which generally come from America and Canada, are usually used for bread-making because of their high gluten content. Durum wheat is a type of hard wheat which is usually used for making pasta. Soft wheats on the other hand are used for cakes and biscuits.

Wholewheat grains, sometimes known as wheatberries, are delicious added to soups, savouries and salads. They have a chewy nutty texture and a wonderful taste.

Cooking method to serve wheatberries instead of rice or mixed into a salad: wash the wheat grains. Bring a pan of water to the boil using 3–4 cups of water per cup of grain. Add the grain and stir once. Cover and cook for 60 minutes or until the grains burst and are soft.

Wheatgerm

The germ of the wheat grain contains all the nutrients which enable the new plant to grow so it's particularly rich in vitamins and minerals. There are two forms of wheatgerm available from health food stores. Raw wheatgerm has the best nutritional content but is liable to go rancid so keep it in the refrigerator. Toasted or stabilised wheatgerm will keep longer and has a pleasant nutty taste. Add it to cereals, stewed fruit, or yoghurt.

Cracked Wheat or Bulgar (Burghul) Wheat

This is a partially cooked wheat product with a delicious nutty flavour. It can be used in place of rice for pilaus, or soaked and used in salads. It can be obtained from health food shops, or Greek groceries and delicatessens under the name pourgouri.

Cooking method: bring the water to the boil using 2 cups of water per cup of grain. Add the grains and simmer for 12–15 minutes. For soaking: use 1½ cups of boiling water per cup of grain and soak the bulgar for 10–15 minutes.

In this chapter I've selected a number of recipes using rice. All of these could be varied by using millet, buckwheat or bulgar wheat instead and you'll find they are equally as delicious. There is also a buckwheat roast, Tibetan Roast, which is quite a classic dish in wholefood cookery, and a favourite of mine, Spiced Savoury Crumble, which will be new to those who have only tried a sweet crumble topping before.

SPICED ALMOND RISOTTO

There is something rather luxurious about almonds and their subtle flavour goes very well with the sweet spices in this dish. I like to eat this with steamed green vegetables and a side salad. It is also delicious served with Gado-Gado Sauce (page 157).

Serves 4
3 tablespoons oil
1 onion, peeled and chopped
1 clove garlic, crushed
6 oz (175 g) long-grain brown rice, washed and drained
3 sticks celery
1 teaspoon cinnamon
1 teaspoon ground coriander
1 teaspoon fresh root ginger, grated
1 pint (570 ml) boiling water
2 oz (50 g) sultanas
4 oz (110 g) mushrooms, wiped and sliced
1 red pepper, de-seeded and cut into strips
4 oz (110 g) blanched almonds
salt and freshly ground black pepper

Garnish:
wedges of lemon with the edges dipped in paprika

Heat the oil in a pan, then add the chopped onion, garlic and drained rice. Fry for 5 minutes turning the mixture over well. Slice the celery diagonally and add it to the pan with the spices and fry for 2–3 minutes. Pour over the boiling water and then add the sultanas, mushrooms, red pepper and almonds – either left whole or roughly chopped. Bring to the boil, cover and simmer for 40 minutes or until the rice is cooked. All the water should by then have been absorbed, but check the risotto constantly during the last 10 minutes of cooking. Season well and serve hot.

SPICED VEGETABLE PILAU

The spices in this pilau include garam masala which is an aromatic mixture of spices which usually includes cardamons, cumin, cinnamon, cloves and black pepper, though the proportions may vary. I buy it ready-made from wholefood stores or Indian shops, but if you find it impossible to get, then use half a teaspoon of ground cumin and half a teaspoon of ground coriander instead.

I like to garnish this pilau with coconut, but you could stir it into the rice instead. You can also use this dish as a basis for a cold curried rice salad to accompany a savoury roast. Otherwise serve it as a main meal with other small side dishes such as chopped cucumber mixed with yoghurt, Spiced Chick Peas (page 127), Creole Pâté (page 42) or Yoghurt and Tahini Dip (page 46).

Serves 3–4

6 oz (175 g) leeks, cleaned and thinly sliced
6 oz (175 g) peas
6 oz (175 g) carrots, scrubbed and diced
2 tablespoons oil
1 teaspoon garam masala
1 teaspoon turmeric
1–1½ teaspoons cayenne pepper
pinch chilli powder
1 clove garlic, crushed
6 oz (175 g) long-grain brown rice
½ pint (275 ml) stock or water
2 oz (50 g) raisins
salt and freshly ground black pepper
1 oz (25 g) coconut

First prepare all the vegetables. Heat the oil, add the spices and fry these for a couple of minutes. Then add the vegetables and the rice and fry the mixture for a further 5 minutes. Add the stock or water, bring to the boil and cook over a gentle heat for 25–30 minutes until the rice is tender. Stir in the raisins and season to taste. Stir in the coconut or, if you prefer, sprinkle it over the top. Transfer to a warm serving dish and serve straight away.

CHINESE-STYLE VEGETABLES WITH RICE

This combination of vegetables is flavoured with soy sauce, ginger and sherry, and uses the quick stir-fry method of cooking to preserve all the freshness in colour and texture of the crisp peppers and crunchy bean sprouts. It's easy to prepare the vegetables while the rice is cooking, so the whole meal will only take about 40 minutes from start to finish. This is particularly good with Flemish Salad (page 188).

Serves 4

8 oz (225 g) long-grain brown rice, washed
18 fl oz (525 ml) boiling water
salt and freshly ground black pepper
3 tablespoons oil
1 teaspoon fresh root ginger, grated
8 oz (225 g) onions, peeled and chopped
1 large red pepper, de-seeded and cut into strips
8 oz (225 g) mushrooms, wiped and sliced
8 oz (225 g) bean sprouts, rinsed
2 tablespoons soy sauce
2 tablespoons sweet sherry
1 rounded teaspoon cornflour dissolved in 1 tablespoon water

First cook the rice by bringing the water to the boil, pouring in the rice, stirring once and allowing the rice to cook until it is just soft. This takes about 25–30 minutes. Then season it lightly to taste.

Meanwhile prepare the vegetables. Heat the oil and fry the ginger and onions for 5 minutes. Then add the pepper and mushrooms and fry for a further 3–5 minutes. Add the bean sprouts and stir, then add the soy sauce, sherry and dissolved cornflour. Cook over a high heat for about 3 minutes, stirring constantly. Drain the rice and then turn it onto a warm serving dish, pile the cooked vegetables over the top and serve straight away.

SAVOURY GOLDEN RICE RING

This dish has a stunning colour and is fruity and refreshing. I serve it in a number of ways, either plain as a salad, or piled into scooped-out pineapple halves topped with fresh or glacé cherries. Alternatively, press it into a ring, surround it with greenery, and pile the centre of the ring high with bunches of grapes. This way it makes an impressive centrepiece for a buffet party.

Serves 6

1 oz (25 g) butter or 1 tablespoon oil
2 teaspoons turmeric
2 large onions, peeled and finely chopped
1 clove garlic, crushed
1 red pepper, de-seeded and diced
9 oz (250 g) cooked short-grain brown rice
1 oz (25 g) crystallised ginger
½ medium-sized pineapple
4 oz (110 g) blanched almonds
3 tablespoons olive oil
1½ tablespoons white wine vinegar
salt and freshly ground black pepper

Heat the butter or oil and fry the turmeric, onions, garlic and red pepper until soft. Stir in the cooked rice and leave the mixture to cool. Finely chop the ginger, pineapple and almonds and add them all to the rice. Combine the olive oil and vinegar, mix this into the rice and season to taste. Then press the mixture firmly into an oiled ring mould. Refrigerate overnight.

To unmould, stand the mould in hot water for a few minutes. Then place a serving plate over the mould and turn both upside down. Tap it firmly and shake it a little, and the rice ring will come out.

CASHEW PAELLA

This dish can be such fun served paella-style. Choose a large round platter or use a skillet, fill it with the paella and go to town on the garnishes. I like to use long-grain rice in this dish as I think it holds its shape and looks better. I suggest you use celery and peppers but of course when courgettes, mushrooms and fresh tomatoes are in season they can all be added for more variety. This paella is delicious served with runner beans, creamed mushrooms, or a green salad.

Serves 4
2 tablespoons oil
1 onion, peeled and finely chopped
1–2 cloves garlic, crushed
4 oz (110 g) long-grain brown rice, washed
3 oz (75 g) cashew nut pieces
$\frac{1}{2}$ teaspoon paprika
2 teaspoons fresh basil or 1 teaspoon dried basil
1 red or green pepper, de-seeded and cut in strips
5 sticks celery, diced
1 pint (570 ml) boiling water
1 × 14 oz (400 g) tin of tomatoes, liquidised or sieved
extra boiling water (if needed)
salt and freshly ground black pepper

Garnish:
black and green olives
lemon wedges
1 hard-boiled egg, sliced

Heat the oil in a frying-pan and fry the onion and garlic for a few minutes. Add the rice along with the cashew nuts, paprika and dried basil and cook for a few minutes, turning the mixture over well so that the rice and nuts are slightly roasted. Add the peppers and celery and mix in.

Pour on 1 pint (570 ml) boiling water and add the liquidised tomatoes. Bring to the boil and simmer uncovered for 35–40 minutes.

If you are using fresh basil, stir it in now. The water content may need checking towards the end of the cooking, but most of the liquid should evaporate leaving a moist mixture with a rich tomato colour. Season well and garnish according to taste.

RISOTTO PIEDMONTAISE

Piedmontaise is the Italian term for unpolished rice often used in risotto. Classic risotto is made with butter, cheese (half Parmesan and half Gruyère) salt, pepper and lemon juice and this is an attractive variation which goes with almost any savoury. I find it interesting to alter the type of cheese used, sometimes substituting a strong Cheddar or Edam for the traditional Parmesan and Gruyère.

Serves 4
2 oz (50 g) butter
8 oz (225 g) long-grain brown rice, washed
1 pint (570 ml) boiling water
4 oz (110 g) cooked peas
4 oz (110 g) mushrooms, wiped and thinly sliced
2 oz (50 g) Parmesan or Cheddar cheese, grated
a little extra butter
3 teaspoons lemon juice
salt and freshly ground black pepper

Melt the butter in a 3 pint (1·75 litre) pan and fry the rice gently for a few minutes. Pour on the boiling water and cook the rice for about 25–30 minutes until it is just tender. The water should have evaporated by this time but if there is any excess, dry out the rice on a high heat. Then add the sliced mushrooms, peas and grated cheese. Stir in and heat through for 5 minutes adding a little extra butter if necessary. Then add the lemon juice and season to taste. Serve straight away.

SPICED SAVOURY CRUMBLE

The crumble topping I like best is one in which I rub in butter or margarine and then add extra fat in the form of oil. I find this gives the crumble topping a crisp, light texture which perfectly balances the braised vegetable filling. In this recipe I've suggested using wholewheat flour and porridge oats. Other flakes and flours may be used instead, such as barley flakes which are sweet and nutty, or rye flakes which are darker with a distinctive tangy flavour. Corn flour will give you a golden topping and rice flour a very finely textured crumble. It is certainly worth experimenting with different combinations.

I often make this dish in the winter, when there is ample choice of root vegetables. Serve with, for example, baked potatoes and steamed cauliflower and Tomato Sauce (page 154).

Serves 4
4 oz (110 g) peas
8 oz (225 g) celery, trimmed and chopped
8 oz (225 g) carrots, scrubbed and diced
8 oz (225 g) courgettes, washed and diced
2 teaspoons cumin
2 teaspoons coriander
1 teaspoon turmeric
½ teaspoon chilli powder
½ teaspoon fresh root ginger, grated
8 oz (225 g) onions, peeled and chopped
1–2 cloves garlic, crushed
2 tablespoons oil
1 tablespoon tomato purée
¾ pint (400 ml) dark vegetable stock
salt and freshly ground black pepper

For the crumble topping:
3 oz (75 g) wholewheat flour
2 oz (50 g) butter or margarine
3 oz (75 g) porridge oats
2 tablespoons oil
salt and freshly ground black pepper

146

Pre-heat the oven to gas mark 5, 375°F (190°C).

First prepare the vegetables. Then mix the spices to a paste with 2–3 tablespoons of water. Heat the oil in a large saucepan and fry the onion and garlic until soft. Then add the spice paste and cook the mixture for 5–8 minutes, stirring frequently. Mix in the diced vegetables and cook for another 2 minutes. Now add the tomato purée, stock, salt and freshly ground black pepper. Bring to the boil, then cover the pan and cook the mixture for 15 minutes on a gentle heat. Transfer the cooked vegetables to a lightly greased 3 pint (1·75 litre) ovenproof dish.

Meanwhile prepare the crumble topping. Put the flour in a small bowl and rub in the butter or margarine. Then stir in the porridge oats and mix in the oil. Season to taste. Sprinkle this mixture over the top of the cooked vegetables and bake the dish for 25–30 minutes. Serve straight away.

TIBETAN ROAST

This dark-coloured roast, flecked with green, can be baked in a loaf tin or ring mould. The main ingredients are barley or buckwheat, walnuts and mushrooms, and the barley or buckwheat is lightly fried first as this brings out the best flavour. The strong taste enhanced by the red wine makes this a rich roast. Serve hot with Mushroom and Sherry Sauce (page 158) and roast vegetables for a warming winter meal.

Serves 4–6
1 teaspoon oil
4 oz (110 g) buckwheat or barley
4 oz (110 g) onions, peeled and finely diced
8 oz (225 g) mushrooms, wiped and chopped
$\frac{1}{4}$ pint (150 ml) red wine
$\frac{1}{4}$ pint (150 ml) stock
4 oz (110 g) walnuts
8 oz (225 g) spinach
2 teaspoons fresh rosemary or 1 teaspoon dried rosemary
2 teaspoons fresh sage or 1 teaspoon dried sage
1 egg
salt and freshly ground black pepper
1 teaspoon butter

Pre-heat the oven to gas mark 5, 375°F (190°C).

Heat the oil and fry the buckwheat or barley for 2–3 minutes allowing it to brown slightly. Then add the onions and continue cooking the mixture for a few minutes. Add the mushrooms and cook for a further 5 minutes with the pan covered. Then pour in the wine and stock and bring the mixture to the boil. Reduce the heat and simmer for about 20 minutes in the case of buckwheat, or 50 minutes in the case of barley, adding a little more stock if necessary.

Meanwhile grind the walnuts finely in a mouli or blender. Prepare the spinach by washing it in several changes of water and cooking it in a heavy-bottomed pan without any water for about 6 minutes. Drain off any excess liquid and chop the spinach thoroughly.

When the buckwheat or barley is cooked, remove the pan from the heat and let the mixture cool slightly. Then stir in the ground walnuts and chopped spinach, rosemary and sage. Mix in the lightly beaten egg and season the mixture well.

Grease a 1 lb (450 g) loaf tin with a teaspoon of butter and then press in the loaf mixture. Bake for 50–60 minutes until the top is a dark brown and feels firm to the touch. If serving this loaf hot, let it stand for 10 minutes before turning it out of the tin. Alternatively it can be eaten cold.

Sauces

Savoury Brown Sauce ❦ White Sauce ❦ Onion Sauce ❦ Tomato Sauce
Red Wine and Tomato Sauce ❦ Barbecue Sauce ❦ Gado-Gado Sauce
Mushroom and Sherry Sauce ❦ Quick Hollandaise Sauce
Oriental Garden Sauce ❦ Sauce Ravigote

I think there is a place for a sauce at almost every meal; it can add interest and substance to the plainest dish. Most take very little time to prepare and can either be made while the main part of the meal is cooking, or can be prepared well in advance and re-heated when needed. When re-heating a sauce it's generally advisable to use a double boiler or improvise one by putting the container into a larger saucepan of hot water set on a gentle heat. This means the sauce will heat through evenly and will not burn at the bottom. Most sauces freeze well unless they are heavily spiced or flavoured with garlic.

Sauces are very important in vegetarian cookery. It is always a good idea to serve one with roasts, croquettes and savoury pastries to counteract any dryness. In this section I've given three standard recipes for hot sauces: White Sauce, Savoury Brown Sauce and Tomato Sauce. Use the standard recipes for everyday meals but do try some of the additional special sauces for entertaining.

SAVOURY BROWN SAUCE

A rich brown sauce made with vegetables, grains or beans is an essential accompaniment for many savoury vegetarian dishes. The best sauces come from using a good, well flavoured stock, such as the juice from stewed mushrooms, or the cooking liquid from red kidney beans or brown lentils. The roux should be cooked to a golden colour as this determines the final colour of the sauce, and extra flavouring is added by using yeast extracts, miso (soya bean paste) or soy sauce. Once you have mastered a good brown sauce, there are plenty of variations to complement any main dish.

Makes ¾ pint (400 ml) sauce
1½ oz (40 g) butter or 1½ tablespoons oil
1 medium onion, peeled and finely chopped
a little salt
½ teaspoon celery seed or 2 sticks of celery, finely chopped
1 oz (25 g) wholewheat flour
½ teaspoon mustard powder
1 pint (570 ml) vegetable or bean stock
1 teaspoon dried thyme or 2 teaspoons fresh thyme, chopped
1 bay leaf
1 teaspoon yeast extract or 1 teaspoon miso (see page 21)
1 teaspoon soy sauce
salt and freshly ground black pepper

Melt the butter over a gentle heat, then fry the onion for 5–7 minutes, sprinkling over a little salt so that the juices in the onion are brought out. Then add the celery seed. Sprinkle over the flour and mustard powder and allow this roux to cook for 3–5 minutes so that it turns a golden brown colour. Then add the stock gradually, stirring constantly, and bring to the boil adding the thyme, bay leaf and flavourings. Let the sauce cook on a gentle heat for 5–7 minutes, then correct the seasonings and continue cooking for a further 10 minutes in a partially covered pan so that the sauce reduces.

BROWN SAUCE JULIENNE

A richer version of the basic Brown Sauce can be made by lightly frying a mixture of finely shredded root vegetables (a julienne) with the onion. Use 2 oz (50 g) of mixed carrot, turnip and swede chopped into small pieces the size and shape of a matchstick. These vegetables can then be strained out at the end of cooking or mashed in if you want a thicker version of the sauce. Cook this sauce for 15 minutes.

BROWN SAUCE WITH MUSHROOMS

Use 4 oz (110 g) field or flat mushrooms. Chop these very finely, fry them with the onion, then continue with the basic Brown Sauce.

WHITE SAUCE

This is a useful sauce which can be the basis for many useful variations. It is important to cook both the roux and the finished sauce well, otherwise it will taste of uncooked flour.

Makes ½ pint (275 ml)
1½ oz (40 g) butter
1 tablespoon flour
½ pint (275 ml) warmed milk
salt and freshly ground black pepper
nutmeg

Melt the butter in a small pan and, when it is foaming, sprinkle over the flour. Cook this over a gentle heat for 2–3 minutes. Then pour on the milk, about one-quarter at a time, stirring well. Remember to go round the edges of the pan to stir in any uncooked roux. When all the milk is added, bring the sauce to boiling point, then simmer on a very gentle heat for 3–5 minutes, stirring all the time. Season and serve straight away, or, if you do not want to serve the sauce immediately, pour a little melted butter over the top. This creates a film which stops a skin from forming.

WHITE SAUCE WITH CHEESE

Add 2–4 oz (50–110 g) grated Cheddar Cheese when the sauce is cooked. Stir it in until it has melted.

WHITE SAUCE WITH HERBS

Add 1–2 tablespoons chopped herbs, such as dill, tarragon or parsley, or $\frac{1}{2}$ tablespoon grated horseradish when the sauce is cooked.

CREAMY WHITE SAUCE

Substitute either cream or light vegetable stock for part of the milk to make a richer or lighter version respectively.

ONION SAUCE

This sauce has the delicate flavour of onions and a creamy consistency. Its subtle mustard seasoning means that it goes well with any of the savoury roasts or with lightly steamed green vegetables.

Makes $\frac{1}{2}$ pint (275 ml) sauce
$\frac{1}{2}$ lb (225 g) onions, peeled and sliced very thinly
$1\frac{1}{2}$ oz (40 g) butter
1 dessertspoon flour
salt, pepper and pinch of nutmeg
$\frac{1}{2}$ pint (275 ml) warm milk
$\frac{1}{2}$ teaspoon mustard powder

Fry the onions gently in the butter until they turn a pale yellow colour. This takes 7–10 minutes. Then stir in the flour and add the seasonings. Pour over the milk, bring the sauce to the boil and then simmer gently for 15 minutes in a covered pan. Let it cool slightly and then purée in a liquidiser for 30 seconds until it has a smooth creamy consistency. Return the pan to the heat, add the mustard powder and re-heat gently, correcting the seasonings. Serve hot.

TOMATO SAUCE

As with a white or brown sauce, a classic tomato sauce is wonderful on its own or it can be the basis for many variations. This one is very versatile and easy to make; it also freezes well. There isn't always time to deal with fresh tomatoes, but a good quality tinned variety is often just as good as long as you buy one where the tomatoes have been canned in their own juice. This sauce is excellent with any type of pasta.

Makes ½ pint (275 ml) sauce
2 tablespoons olive oil
1 large onion, peeled and finely chopped
1 clove garlic, crushed
1½ lb (700 g) fresh tomatoes, skinned and sliced, or 1 × 28 oz (800 g) tin of tomatoes
2 tablespoons tomato purée
2 teaspoons fresh chopped basil or 1 teaspoon dried basil
salt and freshly ground black pepper

Heat the oil in a heavy-bottomed saucepan and gently fry the chopped onion and garlic for 7–10 minutes until they are soft and translucent, taking care not to colour them. Then add the tomatoes, tomato purée, dried basil (if using), salt and freshly ground black pepper to taste. Lower the heat and cook the sauce for 35–40 minutes in a partially covered pan so that it will reduce slightly. If you are using fresh basil add it now. Correct the seasoning and serve. For a smoother texture the sauce can be liquidised and then re-heated before serving.

RED WINE AND TOMATO SAUCE

Make this special sauce for dinner parties and festive occasions to accompany roasts or pastas. It is richer than a basic tomato sauce since it contains red wine, and extra vegetables and herbs.

Makes approximately 1 pint (570 ml) sauce
2 tablespoons olive oil
1 medium onion, peeled and chopped
1 clove garlic, crushed
3 sticks celery, chopped
1 lb (450 g) tomatoes
2 pints (1·1 litres) boiling water
2 tablespoons tomato purée
½ pint (275 ml) water
4 tablespoons red wine, preferably burgundy
1 teaspoon dried thyme
1 teaspoon dried basil
½ teaspoon salt
freshly ground black pepper

Heat the oil in a saucepan, then add the onion and garlic and cook slowly until softened. Do not let the onion colour. Add the celery and cook for a further few minutes. Put the tomatoes into a bowl and pour over the boiling water. Let them stand for a few minutes, then drain, skin and chop. Add these to the pan together with the tomato purée, water, wine and herbs. Season well and simmer uncovered for 30–40 minutes so that the sauce reduces slightly.

BARBECUE SAUCE

I like this version of barbecue sauce as its flavouring is sharp yet subtle — a reminder that a sauce is intended to highlight a dish rather than overpower it. It is quick to make and can be finished off in two different ways. It you strain or sieve the vegetables through a mouli the final result will be a smooth, pouring sauce. Its colour is a brownish red with quite a tangy, lemon flavour. If you purée it in a liquidiser the end result has a redder colour and is thicker. Either way it is delicious and I think it is especially good with the Three Layer Terrine (page 62), Cheese and Lentil Loaf (page 59) or with brown rice.

Makes 1 pint (570 ml) sauce
1 teaspoon oil, preferably olive
1 onion, peeled and finely chopped
1 clove garlic, crushed
1 × 28 oz (800 g) tin of tomatoes, drained
2–3 stalks celery, finely chopped
2–3 thin slices lemon
2½ tablespoons white wine vinegar or cider vinegar
2 tablespoons tomato ketchup
1 tablespoon soy sauce
½ pint (275 ml) fruit juice, preferably apple juice
2 bay leaves
salt and freshly ground black pepper

Heat the oil in a saucepan and gently fry the onion and garlic until soft. Add the remaining ingredients and bring them to the boil. Simmer gently for 20 minutes in a covered pan, remove the bay leaves, then purée the cooked sauce and return it to a clean pan to reheat. It will not need thickening. If you prefer a smoother version, sieve the vegetables or press them through a mouli then return the sauce to a clean pan. Season and serve hot.

GADO-GADO SAUCE

The inspiration for this recipe comes from Indonesia and it is extremely simple to make. I've found it a useful sauce for accompanying many dishes, e.g. Plain Brown Rice (page 137), or more elaborate dishes such as Spiced Almond Risotto (page 140) or Cheese and Lentil Loaf (page 59). Gado-Gado Sauce is based on peanut butter so it has a nutty flavour and a golden brown colour. This recipe makes a pouring sauce, but you can make thicker, richer versions if you use more peanut butter and substitute milk for some of the stock. Once you've tried this sauce I'm sure it will be a permanent feature of your repertoire.

Makes 1½ pints (900 ml) sauce
2 tablespoons oil
1 large onion, peeled and finely chopped
1 clove garlic, crushed
1 bay leaf
1–2 teaspoons root ginger, finely grated
½ teaspoon salt
6–8 tablespoons peanut butter
1 tablespoon honey
juice of 1 lemon
1 tablespoon white wine vinegar or cider vinegar
1–1½ pints (570–900 ml) water
¼ teaspoon cayenne pepper
salt and freshly ground black pepper
1 teaspoon soy sauce

Heat the oil in a medium-sized saucepan and gently fry the chopped onion, garlic, bay leaf and ginger, sprinkling in ½ teaspoon salt while frying to bring out the juices and make the onion more succulent. When the onions become translucent add all the remaining ingredients and mix them together very thoroughly. At first the sauce will look fairly thin but as the water heats up the peanut butter will gradually thicken and the sauce will become creamier and thicker as it cooks. Bring to the boil, then simmer on a very low heat for 20 minutes, stirring occasionally. Check the seasoning before serving.

MUSHROOM AND SHERRY SAUCE

This rich sauce is especially suitable for dinner parties and special occasions. I often find people miss gravy more than anything else when they become totally vegetarian and if you are in this situation, do try this sauce — it's much more delicious than gravy ever was!

Makes 1¼ pints (550 ml) sauce
1 oz (25 g) butter
8 oz (225 g) mushrooms, wiped and quartered
1 tablespoon sherry
4 teaspoons flour
1 pint (570 ml) strong vegetable stock
salt and freshly ground black pepper

Melt the butter in a saucepan and add the mushrooms and sherry. Cover and cook for 2–3 minutes on a high heat. Uncover and continue to cook until the liquid evaporates, stirring constantly, so that the mushrooms are well browned. Reduce the heat, add the flour and cook it thoroughly for 5–6 minutes, stirring all the time. Add the stock a little at a time, stirring constantly to prevent lumps forming. Simmer for 3–5 minutes and then season to taste. Let the sauce cool slightly, then liquidise until it is smooth. Gently re-heat the sauce in a clean pan.

QUICK HOLLANDAISE SAUCE

Hollandaise Sauce is so rich, delicious and versatile it's worth having a recipe that can be made quickly and which is a sure-fire success. A liquidiser does make this recipe very quick and easy. This is a sauce which is particularly delicious with hot broccoli, sautéed courgettes or steamed green beans.

Serves 4
4 oz (110 g) butter
3 egg yolks
2 tablespoons lemon juice or wine vinegar
$\frac{1}{8}$ teaspoon salt
pinch cayenne pepper

Melt the butter gently in a small saucepan. Place the remaining ingredients in a liquidiser and blend for 15 seconds. When the butter has melted pour it in a slow stream over the other ingredients and liquidise thoroughly. Serve immediately or keep warm over hot water.

If you don't have a blender, heat the lemon juice or vinegar with the cayenne in a small pan and simmer until the liquid is reduced by half. Let the pan cool. Add the egg yolks, whisking all the time, then heat the mixture in a double boiler over a low heat until it begins to thicken. Melt the butter and whisk it into the thickened sauce. Season to taste.

ORIENTAL GARDEN SAUCE

This sauce, which is really a cross between a sauce and a chutney, may be made with apples or plums depending on the season. Leave the fruit in chunky pieces as this gives the best texture, and serve this sauce cold as an accompaniment to brown rice, or savoury roasts such as Layered Cashew and Mushroom Roast (page 60). It will keep well for up to a week in the refrigerator.

Makes $\frac{1}{2}$ pint (275 ml) sauce
12 oz (350 g) cooking apples or plums
6 tablespoons water
2 tablespoons cider vinegar
1 tablespoon brown sugar
2 teaspoons soy sauce
$\frac{1}{2}$ teaspoon root ginger, freshly grated
1 clove garlic, crushed

Wash and core the apples, or stone the plums, leaving the fruit unpeeled, and cut them into large pieces. Put all the ingredients together in a large, covered saucepan and bring the mixture to the boil. Turn the heat down and continue cooking over a gentle heat until the fruit is soft and the flavours are well blended. This takes about 30 minutes. Let the sauce cool completely before serving.

SAUCE RAVIGOTE

Serve this sharp sauce with flans, salads or savouries. Being bright green it provides good colour contrast. The true meaning of ravigote is to refresh, and certainly the sharp flavours add zest to strong and mild dishes.

2 oz (50 g) parsley and watercress
1 bunch spring onions
1 tablespoon capers
2–3 gherkins
8 tablespoons olive oil
1 teaspoon vinegar
squeeze of lemon juice

Trim the stalks from the parsley and watercress and chop the leaves finely. Then clean the spring onions and chop finely. Mix these together in a bowl, then add the chopped capers and sliced gherkins. Mix in the olive oil with vinegar and lemon juice to taste. Let the sauce stand for an hour or so before serving.

Accompanying Vegetables

Aubergines Parmesan 🐸 Stuffed Aubergines
Broccoli in Lemon Cream Sauce 🐸 Stuffed Cabbage Leaves in Cider Sauce
Spiced Somerset Carrots 🐸 Stuffed Courgettes
Leek and Mushroom Gratin 🐸 Baked Onions with Sherry
Parsnip Croquettes 🐸 Stuffed Peppers 🐸 Baked Potatoes
Paprika Potatoes 🐸 Cheese Potatoes with Caraway 🐸 Ratatouille
Sprouts à la Brigoule 🐸 Buttered Spinach 🐸 Mixed Vegetable Nitsuke
Crisp Green Stir-fry 🐸 Spiced Chinese Stir-fry

At home it is possible to cook vegetables properly and enjoy them at their best. It seems to be very rare, however, for a restaurant to serve fresh vegetables cooked to order so that they are just right. Vegetables should, of course, be as fresh as possible and should generally be undercooked, preferably by steaming or baking. I also like to buy organically grown vegetables whenever I can as I think they have a much better flavour.

Many dishes in this section can be eaten as a separate course; Broccoli in Lemon Cream Sauce or Ratatouille both make delicious starters. When planning a meal, if you have a lot of vegetables to chop up for the main course, pick a fairly plain vegetable recipe such as Buttered Spinach or Somerset Glazed Carrots to serve with it. Use pasta or rice as an accompaniment because they, too, need very little preparation.

Some of the other dishes given here could be served as a main course, such as Cheese and Potatoes with Caraway or Aubergines Parmesan. Stuffed vegetables are also excellent main course dishes and I have included recipes for Stuffed Cabbage, Peppers and Courgettes, all of which are delicious.

AUBERGINES PARMESAN

This is one of my favourite dishes; it is rich and colourful yet simple to make and very satisfying to eat. Look for aubergines with glossy skins free from any brown patches which would indicate that they are spoiling. Don't buy ones with wrinkled skins; they should be tight so that the flesh is firm underneath.

Some people find that aubergines are slightly bitter. To remove the bitterness, slice the aubergines, which need not be peeled, and sprinkle them with salt. Leave them to stand, then wash and pat dry before frying. This dish is good served with Mixed Green Salad (page 184) and Plain Brown Rice (page 137).

Serves 4–5
¼ pint (150 ml) olive oil
1 onion, peeled and finely chopped
2 cloves garlic, crushed
1 × 28 oz (800 g) tin of tomatoes, drained
2 tablespoons tomato purée
2 teaspoons fresh chopped basil or 1 teaspoon dried basil
salt and freshly ground black pepper
1¼ lb (550 g) aubergines, unpeeled
salt
8 oz (225 g) mozzarella or Cheddar cheese
3 tablespoons Parmesan cheese

Pre-heat the oven to gas mark 4, 350°F (180°C).

First make the sauce. Heat 1 tablespoon of the olive oil in a saucepan and gently fry the finely chopped onion and crushed garlic for 5 to 7 minutes so they remain juicy. Then add the tomatoes, tomato purée, basil, salt and pepper, cover the pan and let this mixture simmer on a very low heat for 30 minutes, stirring occasionally.

Wash the aubergines and cut them into slices about ¼ inch (½ cm) thick. Put them on a large plate, lightly salt them and then leave them for 20 minutes so that any bitter juices are drawn out. After this, rinse and pat dry. Heat some more olive oil in a deep frying-pan and fry the slices a few at a time so that they become soft and are lightly browned. Drain them on kitchen paper. If all the oil is used during the cooking add a little more to the pan.

Next lightly oil a 3 pint (1·75 litre) ovenproof dish and pour in a little of the tomato sauce. Then make a layer of one-third of the aubergine slices followed by a layer of sliced mozzarella cheese or grated Cheddar cheese and then some more sauce. Repeat these layers ending with a topping of sauce, and cover that with the Parmesan cheese. Cover the dish with foil or a matching lid and bake it for 20 minutes in the centre of the oven. Then uncover it and bake for a further 10–15 minutes so that the cheese browns nicely on top and serve straight away.

STUFFED AUBERGINES

Cheese and mushrooms make a delicious filling for aubergines which when baked turn a rich brown colour. This dish goes well with Tomato Sauce (page 154), a bright green vegetable such as broccoli and plain brown rice.

Serves 4
4 medium-sized aubergines
6 oz (175 g) onions, peeled and finely chopped
6 oz (175 g) mushrooms, wiped and finely chopped
6 oz (175 g) Cheddar cheese, grated
2 teaspoons finely chopped fresh marjoram or 1 teaspoon dried marjoram
¼ teaspoon cayenne pepper
2 eggs
salt and freshly ground black pepper
extra oil for brushing filling
1 quantity of Savoury Brown Sauce (page 151)

Pre-heat the oven to gas mark 4, 350°F (180°C).

Cut the aubergine in half lengthways and scoop out the flesh with a teaspoon, taking care not to split the skins and leaving a shell ¼ inch (½ cm) thick. Blanch the shells for 5 minutes in boiling water.

Now prepare the onions, mushrooms and cheese and mix them all together in a large bowl. Mix in the chopped aubergine flesh, marjoram and cayenne pepper. Beat the eggs and add to the aubergine filling, mixing them in thoroughly. Then season to taste. Pile some filling into each of the aubergine shells and lay them in a lightly oiled oven-to-table dish. Pour in the Savoury Brown Sauce and brush the filling with some extra oil. Cover the dish with foil or a matching lid and bake for 40 minutes or until the shells are tender and the topping is dark brown. Serve straight away.

BROCCOLI IN
LEMON CREAM SAUCE

Broccoli is a member of the cabbage family and is a close relation of the cauliflower. There is the purple-headed or 'purple sprouting' type and also the green-headed variety which is known as calabrese. You can use either in this dish. Buy broccoli where the heads are closely packed together as those breaking into flower can be rather woody and tasteless. The sauce has a subtle lemon tang and can be made just before the broccoli is cooked and kept warm over a pan of hot water.

Serves 4 as a side vegetable
1 lb (450 g) broccoli
1½ oz (40 g) butter
2 rounded teaspoons flour
8 fl oz (225 ml) single cream or milk
2 egg yolks
2 tablespoons lemon juice
salt and freshly ground black pepper

Garnish:
crushed coriander seeds or coarsely ground black pepper

Prepare the broccoli by dividing it into even-sized heads or spears and trimming the base of each stalk; split the thicker stalks to ensure even cooking.

Melt ½ oz (10 g) butter in a pan; add the flour and cook this roux for 1–2 minutes. Add the milk gradually and bring the sauce to the boil, stirring constantly. Then remove the pan from the heat. Beat the egg yolks in a small bowl and mix in a little of the sauce. Add this to the rest of the sauce, stirring well. Transfer the mixture to a double-boiler. Return to the heat and stir in the remaining butter and lemon juice. Heat the sauce gently until it begins to thicken. Season to taste.

Meanwhile steam or cook the broccoli in a very small amount of boiling salted water for about 5–7 minutes. When it is cooked, put it into a warm serving dish, pour the sauce over the top and garnish with a few crushed coriander seeds or coarsely ground black pepper. Serve straight away.

STUFFED CABBAGE LEAVES IN CIDER SAUCE

This is a delicious supper dish which looks impressive but is easy to make. The secret of success lies in the choice of cabbage leaves. Choose medium-sized leaves which will hold about 1–1¼ tablespoons of filling and look for leaves of a good even colour. The January King and Savoy varieties of cabbage are the best. Use inner and outer leaves for variety and try the Spiced Almond Risotto (page 140) as an alternative filling. I like to serve this with Spiced Somerset Carrots (page 167).

Serves 4
3 tablespoons oil
8 oz (225 g) onions, peeled and finely chopped
1 teaspoon crushed coriander seeds
¼ lb (110 g) long-grain brown rice
½ pt (275 ml) boiling water
2 oz (50 g) chopped, blanched almonds or pine kernels
2 tablespoons dark seedless raisins
salt and freshly ground black pepper
juice of 1 lemon
12 cabbage leaves
¼ pt (150 ml) cider
¼ pt (150 ml) stock
1 bay leaf
2 teaspoons cornflour
Garnish:
4 slices of lemon
1 tablespoon flaked almonds, lightly toasted

Pre-heat the oven to gas mark 4, 350°F (180°C).

Heat the oil in a frying-pan and add the finely chopped onion and crushed coriander seeds. Cook this gently for 5–7 minutes. Wash and drain the rice, then add it to the frying-pan. Stir constantly, letting the grains toast slightly for 1–2 minutes. Then pour on the boiling water and add the finely chopped almonds or pine kernels and the seedless raisins. Cover the pan and cook this mixture until the rice is tender, which takes about 40–45 minutes. Check on the amount of liquid about 10 minutes before the end of cooking and should you need more, add boiling water, but only a little at a time. Season the rice and add the lemon juice to taste.

Select medium-sized cabbage leaves and blanch them a few at a time in a little boiling water. Then place about a tablespoon of the rice mixture onto each leaf and roll each one up neatly. Place them seam-side down in a lightly oiled dish. Pour over the cider and stock and add the bay leaf. Cover the dish with a matching lid or foil and bake for 45 minutes. At the end of cooking, transfer the stuffed leaves onto a warm serving dish. Remove the bay leaf from the remaining liquid and thicken with a little cornflour. Pour the thickened sauce over the top of the leaves and garnish with slices of lemon and a few toasted flaked almonds. Serve immediately.

SPICED SOMERSET CARROTS

Carrots have the advantage of being both cheap and available most of the year round. Also this colourful vegetable can be served in many different ways. In this dish their natural sweetness is complemented by the cider and an extra tang is given with mustard and rosemary. Much of the goodness of carrots lies just below the skin so either scrub them thoroughly, or peel them only very lightly. Serve with Layered Cashew and Mushroom Roast (page 60) or Tibetan Roast (page 147).

Serves 4
1 lb (450 g) carrots, scrubbed
1 oz (25 g) butter
3 fl oz (75 ml) cider
3 fl oz (75 ml) water
2 teaspoons fresh chopped rosemary or 1 teaspoon dried rosemary
1 teaspoon mustard powder

First chop the carrots into dice. Then melt the butter in a small saucepan, add the carrots and cook over a gentle heat for 5 minutes. Pour in the cider and water. Add the rosemary and mustard, bring the liquid to the boil and then simmer in a covered pan for 10 minutes. Check half-way through the cooking time that there is enough liquid. When the carrots are tender, put them in a warm serving dish and boil the remaining liquid until it is thick and syrupy. Pour this as a glaze over the top. Serve straight away.

STUFFED COURGETTES

Courgette is the French word for a small marrow. Sometimes sold under their Italian name, zucchini, they are good value during the summer months. The larger varieties of courgette do sometimes have a tough skin which will need peeling, but otherwise leave the skins on. A rich celery and tomato sauce is the basis of the filling for this dish and I like to serve it with Tomato Sauce (page 154) and brown rice or pasta.

Serves 4

4 large courgettes
8 oz (225 g) onions, peeled and finely chopped
2 tablespoons oil
1 clove garlic, crushed
2 sticks celery, washed and finely chopped
1 × 14 oz (400 g) tin of tomatoes, drained
2 tablespoons fresh parsley, finely chopped
salt and freshly ground black pepper
4 oz (110 g) grated cheese
3–4 tablespoons stock or water

Pre-heat the oven to gas mark 4, 350°F (180°C).

First prepare the courgettes. Wipe and blanch them for 5 minutes in boiling water. Then cut them in half lengthways, scoop out the flesh and chop it finely. Now prepare the onions and lightly fry them in the oil for 2 or 3 minutes. Add the garlic and fry for a further 2–3 minutes. Next add the celery and continue cooking the vegetables for about 5 minutes. Then add the tomatoes, parsley and chopped courgette flesh. Cook this mixture uncovered, stirring occasionally, until it has reduced to a thick rich sauce. (This takes about 20 minutes.) Season well. Let the mixture cool slightly and then pile it into the prepared courgette shells. Place the filled shells in a lightly greased ovenproof dish and sprinkle them with grated cheese. Pour in a little stock or water, then bake for 20 minutes or until the shells are tender and the cheese on top is golden brown and bubbling. Serve straight away.

LEEK AND MUSHROOM GRATIN

The flavours of leeks and wine blend together especially well in this supper dish which could be served with Cheese and Lentil Loaf (page 59), Three Layer Terrine (page 62) or as a main course if accompanied by baked potatoes and simple bean casserole.

Serves 4
1 lb (450 g) leeks, cleaned, trimmed and sliced
4 oz (110 g) mushrooms, wiped and sliced
1 tablespoon oil
$\frac{1}{2}$ pint (275 ml) stock or water
1 bay leaf
1 sprig parsley
juice of $\frac{1}{2}$ lemon
4 oz (110 g) grated Cheddar cheese
$\frac{1}{4}$ pint (150 ml) single cream or milk
2–3 tablespoons white wine
salt and freshly ground black pepper
2 oz fresh brown breadcrumbs
1 tablespoon oil

Pre-heat the oven to gas mark 6, 400°F (200°C).

First prepare the vegetables. Then heat the oil in a small saucepan and fry the vegetables very lightly to seal in the flavour. Pour in the stock or water, bay leaf and lemon juice and cook this uncovered for about 10 minutes. Then lift the vegetables from the pan with a slotted spoon and transfer to a lightly greased ovenproof dish. Boil up the remaining liquid and reduce it until you are left with ¼ pint (150 ml). Next, sprinkle half the cheese over the leeks and mushrooms in the ovenproof dish. Mix together the reduced stock with the cream and wine and season to taste. Pour this mixture over the vegetables. Mix the remaining cheese and breadcrumbs with a tablespoon of oil and sprinkle this over the top of the vegetables to form a crunchy topping. Bake this dish for 15–20 minutes until the top is brown and crispy.

BAKED ONIONS WITH SHERRY

Onions are versatile vegetables which can be used cooked or raw in many dishes but they are equally as good on their own. They are supposed to aid digestion and are also reputed, along with garlic, to help in curing colds. Peeling onions without tears can be quite a trial. I find doing this under a running cold tap solves the problem for me, though I've heard of many other peculiar remedies. For this recipe use onions which are firm and hard with a crisp skin. Serve with a savoury roast or Lentil Croquettes with Parsley Sauce (page 130).

Serves 6
6 large onions
6 cloves
1 tablespoon oil, preferably olive
1 glass medium sherry
salt and freshly ground black pepper
Garnish:
1 tablespoon capers (optional)

Pre-heat the oven to gas mark 6, 400°F (200°C).

Peel the onions and stick each one with a clove. Heat the oil in a flameproof oven dish and fry the whole onions for 2 or 3 minutes. When the oil begins to sizzle, pour in the sherry and boil fiercely for 2 or 3 minutes. Then add extra water so that the liquid comes half-way up the onions. Put the dish in the oven and bake for 1 hour.

Remove the cloves and transfer the onions onto a warm serving dish. Reduce the remaining sauce slightly then pour it around the onions and sprinkle with the capers, salt and freshly ground black pepper. Serve straight away.

PARSNIP CROQUETTES

You can make this dish with a variety of root vegetables as they all make excellent purées and are delicious when served as croquettes. The mixture can be prepared well in advance and used when needed. Parsnips were once eaten on penitential days such as Ash Wednesday, which is perhaps why they have become such a neglected vegetable. Serve these croquettes with a cheese sauce and salad for a light main course, or as an accompanying vegetable for a bean casserole, Winter Vegetable Pie (page 111) or a savoury roast.

Makes 12 small croquettes
1 lb (450 g) parsnips or swedes
12 fl oz (330 ml) milk
1 oz (25 g) butter
2–3 tablespoons snipped chives or shallots, very finely chopped
1 small egg
2 tablespoons flour
salt and freshly ground black pepper
For coating:
1 egg white
4 oz (110 g) fresh brown breadcrumbs

Scrub or peel the parsnips, dice finely and put them into a saucepan with the milk. Bring to the boil, then simmer uncovered until the parsnips are tender and most of the liquid has been absorbed. Drain away any excess milk keeping it for a soup or sauce, then mash the parsnips and add the butter, chives or shallots, beaten egg and flour. Season well and chill the mixture until it is firm.

When required, shape the mixture into croquettes, dip each one in egg white and roll it in breadcrumbs. Deep-fry or shallow-fry the croquettes for about 5 minutes until they are crispy brown on the outside and heated through to the centre. Serve straight away.

STUFFED PEPPERS

Peppers seem to have been specially designed to hold a savoury stuffing and they are very easy to prepare. Red and green peppers are now widely available, and yellow and white varieties are being introduced. Each type has its own distinctive taste. This recipe with its brown rice and mushroom filling and rich tomato sauce is a complete meal on its own.

Serves 4
4 oz (110 g) long-grain brown rice
$\frac{1}{2}$ pint (275 ml) water

For the sauce:
2 onions, peeled and finely chopped
2 cloves garlic, crushed
4 tablespoons oil (preferably olive oil)
2 × 14 oz (400 g) tins of tomatoes
4 tablespoons tomato purée
salt and freshly ground black pepper

4 green peppers

For the stuffing:
1 tablespoon oil
1 large onion, peeled and finely chopped
4 oz (110 g) button mushrooms, wiped and sliced
2 teaspoons fresh chopped thyme or 1 teaspoon dried thyme
1 teaspoon soy sauce

Pre-heat the oven to gas mark 4, 350°F (180°C).

First prepare the rice by washing it in a sieve under a running tap. Bring the water to the boil. When it is boiling add the drained rice, stir once and then turn the heat down to a simmer. Partially cover the pan and simmer for 25–30 minutes until the rice is just cooked and chewy. Check on the water content about 10 minutes before the end of cooking. If you need to add more water always use boiling water and only add a little at a time.

Now prepare the sauce. Fry the finely chopped onion and crushed garlic in the olive oil for about 5 minutes. Add the tomatoes and tomato purée and simmer this for about 30 minutes in a covered pan while the rice is cooking. Season well.

Meanwhile prepare the peppers. Slice off the tops (reserving them for lids) and de-seed them carefully, then blanch in boiling water for 5 minutes. Heat 1 tablespoon of oil in a frying-pan and gently fry the onion for a few minutes. Add the sliced mushrooms and thyme and cook on a low heat for a few minutes. When the rice is cooked, drain away any excess water and mix with the fried onions and mushrooms. Season well with salt, freshly ground black pepper and a little soy sauce. Then fill each pepper with some of the mixture, and replace the lids.

Stand the filled peppers in a lightly oiled, deep ovenproof dish and pour the tomato sauce round the peppers. Cover the dish with foil or a matching lid and bake the peppers for 30 minutes until they are tender but not limp. Serve immediately.

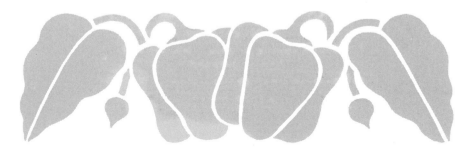

173

BAKED POTATOES

Baked potatoes are delicious either served plain, or split open and covered with grated cheese, yoghurt or soured cream. If you feel it's a little extravagant to use the oven for over an hour just for potatoes, you can scrub them and boil them whole for 20 minutes, then brush them over with oil and let them crisp up in a hot oven for 10–15 minutes. Here are three savoury fillings which make baked potatoes into an extra special dish. Each recipe makes enough filling for four large potatoes.

TO PREPARE THE POTATOES

Pre-heat the oven to gas mark 6, 400°F (200°C).

Scrub the potatoes, brush them over with oil and prick them with a fork. Set on a greased baking tray and bake them in the oven for $1\frac{1}{4}$–$1\frac{1}{2}$ hours.

Meanwhile prepare whichever filling you have chosen.

CHEESE FILLING

2 egg yolks
2 oz (50 g) butter
2 fl oz (50 ml) milk
2 tablespoons grated Cheddar cheese
2 teaspoons parsley, finely chopped
salt and cayenne pepper

Mix up the egg yolks, butter, milk, grated cheese and parsley in a small bowl and season to taste with the salt and cayenne pepper.

ONION AND CREAM CHEESE FILLING

6–8 oz (175–225 g) cream cheese
1 bunch spring onions, cleaned and finely chopped
1 tablespoon fresh parsley, finely chopped
a little milk

Beat all the ingredients together in a small bowl.

EGG AND MUSHROOM FILLING

1 medium onion, peeled and very finely chopped
1 clove garlic, crushed
4 oz (110 g) mushrooms, wiped and finely chopped
1 oz (25 g) butter
2 hard-boiled eggs, shelled and finely chopped
3–4 tablespoons milk
1 tablespoon lemon juice
salt and freshly ground pepper

Lightly sauté the finely chopped onion, garlic and mushrooms in the butter for about 5 minutes. Then remove the pan from the heat and mix in the chopped hard-boiled eggs and moisten the mixture with milk and lemon juice. Season to taste.

TO STUFF THE POTATOES

When the potatoes are cooked, slice them in half lengthwise. Scoop out the flesh leaving a shell $\frac{1}{4}$ inch ($\frac{1}{2}$ cm) thick and mash the potato flesh into the filling mixture. Pile the mixture back into the shells. If you wish, cover with some grated cheese. Put the filled potatoes back into the oven for a further 10–15 minutes. Serve straight away.

PAPRIKA POTATOES

This simple dish is warming to eat and to look at. Paprika comes from grinding sweet red peppers of which the Hungarian type is one of the most well known. Unlike the other red peppers — cayenne and chilli — paprika can be used in quite liberal quantities as it is not very hot at all. Hungarian gulyas or goulash is the famous dish where this spice is used, garnished traditionally with soured cream. This is my version of that dish which I like to serve with green salad for a light supper, or you could make a smaller quantity to accompany a savoury roast.

Serves 4
1 lb (450 g) potatoes, scrubbed and thinly sliced
1 lb (450 g) leeks, cleaned and sliced thinly
12 oz (350 g) mushrooms, wiped and quartered
2 tablespoons oil
$\frac{1}{2}$ tablespoon paprika
salt and freshly ground black pepper
Garnish:
$\frac{1}{4}$ pint (150 ml) soured cream

First prepare all the vegetables. Parboil the potatoes for 12 minutes, then drain, reserving the cooking liquid. Heat the oil and gently fry the leeks, mushrooms and paprika for 8–10 minutes in a covered pan over a gentle heat. This will extract quite a lot of juice from the mushrooms. Then add the parboiled potatoes and mix well, but be careful not to break down the vegetables too much. Continue cooking the vegetables for 5 minutes, adding a little of the potato stock if necessary. Season to taste and serve the dish immediately, topped with lashings of soured cream.

CHEESE POTATOES WITH CARAWAY

Serve this supper dish with a green vegetable or Classic Tomato Salad (page 186) for a quick and easy meal.

Serves 4
2 lb (900 g) potatoes, scrubbed and sliced thinly
2 onions, peeled and sliced
2 cloves garlic, crushed
$\frac{1}{2}$ pint (275 ml) milk
1 teaspoon caraway seeds
1 tablespoon fresh parsley, finely chopped
salt and freshly ground black pepper
4 oz (110 g) grated cheese

Pre-heat the oven to gas mark 4, 350°F (180°C).

Put the potatoes, onions, garlic, milk and caraway seeds into a saucepan and bring them to the boil, then simmer gently for 5 minutes. Gently stir in the parsley and season the mixture to taste. Lightly oil a 3 pint (1·75 litre) ovenproof dish, pour in the mixture and cover with the grated cheese. Bake for 35–40 minutes or until the potatoes are cooked and the cheese is golden brown and bubbling.

RATATOUILLE

Ratatouille is a classic dish as far as both traditional and vegetarian cooks are concerned. The best ratatouille is made when the vegetable flavours are well blended, and the vegetables are soft but not mushy. This can be served as a side vegetable with Cheese and Lentil Loaf (page 59) or Mushroom Flan (page 110). I also like to serve it cold, strongly flavoured with herbs, as a salad dish.

Serves 4
6 tablespoons oil, preferably olive
2 small onions, peeled and finely chopped
2 cloves garlic, crushed
2 small aubergines, unpeeled and chopped into cubes
8 oz (225 g) courgettes, washed and sliced
2 large green or red peppers, de-seeded and diced
8 oz (225 g) tomatoes, roughly chopped
1 tablespoon tomato purée
salt and freshly ground black pepper to taste

Heat the oil in a large saucepan and gently fry the onions and garlic for 5–7 minutes so they become translucent. Meanwhile prepare all the other vegetables and add them to the pan with the tomato purée. Cover and cook the whole mixture over a gentle heat for 30–35 minutes until the vegetables are soft but not mushy. Season to taste. Serve immediately, or leave to cool and serve cold as a salad.

SPROUTS À LA BRIGOULE

One of my favourite vegetables is Brussels sprouts, especially that classic combination, sprouts served with chestnuts. In this recipe the sprouts and chestnuts are baked together in their own sauce. As it is a dish that needs no attention once in the oven it is a very useful one to choose when planning an otherwise complex dinner party menu. This recipe would go well with Layered Cashew and Mushroom Roast (page 60), Red Cabbage Ragout (page 65) or Tibetan Roast (page 147), served with roast potatoes.

Serves 4–6
3 oz (75 g) dried chestnuts or 6 oz (175 g) fresh chestnuts
2 pints (1·1 litres) water
1 lb (450 g) Brussels sprouts
4 oz (110 g) carrot, scrubbed and chopped
1 small onion, peeled and finely chopped
¾ pint (425 ml) stock or water
2 oz (50 g) butter
1 oz (25 g) wholewheat flour
salt and freshly ground black pepper
3 slices of lemon

Pre-heat the oven to gas mark 4, 350°F (180°C).

If you are using dried chestnuts boil them in 2 pints (1·1 litres) of water in a covered pan for 40 minutes or until they are fairly soft. Keep the cooking liquid for the stock. Clean and chop the sprouts in half. Chop the carrot and onion very finely and cook them in the stock for 10 minutes, adding the Brussels sprouts during the last few minutes of cooking. Put the cooked or fresh chestnuts, vegetables and stock into an ovenproof dish. Mix the butter with the flour and stir this into the vegetables. Bring the mixture to the boil, then season to taste and put the slices of lemon in amongst the vegetables. Cover with foil or a matching lid and bake for 25 to 30 minutes.

BUTTERED SPINACH

Spinach was introduced to Europe from Asia in the 16th century and it is a vegetable that is rich in vitamins and minerals. To preserve all this goodness, cook the spinach quickly using no water.

Serves 4
2 lb (900 g) fresh spinach
½ oz (10 g) butter
¼–½ teaspoon freshly grated nutmeg
salt and freshly ground black pepper

Garnish:
fried croûtons of bread

Pick the spinach over, discarding any wilted or coarse leaves. Wash thoroughly in several changes of water. Shake off as much excess water as possible and put the leaves into a heavy-bottomed pan. Cover and cook the spinach over a gentle heat for 6–8 minutes. Drain away any water at the end of the cooking period and then return the spinach to the clean pan and, over a gentle heat, melt in the butter. Season with nutmeg, salt and freshly ground black pepper. Turn the spinach into a warm serving dish and surround it with fried croûtons of bread. Serve immediately.

MIXED VEGETABLE NITSUKE

This is a Japanese name for a sautéed preparation of vegetables in which the vegetables are first lightly sautéed and then steamed or cooked in a little water to which soy sauce or miso has usually been added. This is an excellent way of cooking root vegetables. The Japanese pay great attention to the way in which a vegetable is cut both because they consider the visual appeal of food to be very important and also because uniformly cut pieces ensure even cooking. Different vegetables may be cut into rectangles, rings, strips, half-moons or matchsticks and it is fascinating to experiment and give vegetables an entirely different look by cutting them in a new way. Try serving these vegetables with Tibetan Roast (page 147), or Cheese and Lentil Loaf (page 59).

Serves 3–4
12 oz (350 g) green beans cut into 1 inch (2·5 cm) pieces
12 oz (350 g) leeks, cleaned and chopped
12 oz (350 g) cauliflower, washed and divided into small florets
2 tablespoons oil
1 teaspoon fresh root ginger, grated
2 tablespoons soy sauce
1 tablespoon honey
2 tablespoons white wine or sherry
4 tablespoons water

First prepare all the vegetables. Then heat the oil, fry the root ginger for a few seconds and add the beans, leeks and cauliflower. Cook these for 5 minutes over a high heat, stirring constantly. Mix together the soy sauce, honey, white wine or sherry and water and pour these over the vegetables. Cover the pan and let them simmer for a further 10 minutes or until just tender. Serve straight away.

STIR-FRY VEGETABLES

The stir-fry technique is very popular in Chinese cookery and means just what it says — to stir and fry simultaneously. This is not very different from sauté cooking but more heat and less oil are used. The wok is the traditional vessel for stir-fry cooking. It is a thin metal pan with a rounded bottom and its shape ensures that the heat is evenly distributed and gives as large an area as possible for cooking all the ingredients quickly. You can use a large frying-pan instead. The preparation of the ingredients takes a while as they must all be ready before the cooking starts. Once that begins it is only a matter of minutes from start to finish. It is fun chopping the vegetables, using all the variations of shredding, slicing, dicing and grating in order to get variety.

Groundnut oil is one of the most popular oils for frying, but soya or sunflower oil are often used instead. Sesame seed oil with its distinctive flavour is generally sprinkled over dishes before serving and treated as a seasoning.

When stir-frying, use a high heat and put in first the vegetables which will take the longest time to cook. The flavourings should be added last to enhance the aroma and taste. Liquid flavourings such as soy sauce and sherry generate a burst of steam which finishes cooking the vegetables. This style of cooking needn't always have a Chinese flavour. Also different vegetable combinations can be cooked together quite simply.

CRISP GREEN STIR-FRY

Serves 3–4

1 tablespoon oil
1 lb (450 g) spring green cabbage, finely shredded
4 oz (110 g) peas
2 oz (50 g) bean sprouts
2 teaspoons sugar
2 teaspoons red wine vinegar
2 teaspoons soy sauce
a little sesame oil (optional)

Prepare the vegetables. Then heat the oil in a wok or large skillet and when it is very hot add the cabbage, peas and bean sprouts and stir furiously for 3 minutes. Mix together the sugar, vinegar and soy sauce and pour this over the vegetables. Cook on a high heat for a further minute. Then sprinkle with a little sesame oil and serve immediately.

SPICED CHINESE STIR-FRY

Serves 3–4

8 oz (225 g) spring onions, trimmed and chopped
8 oz (225 g) mushrooms, wiped and quartered
8 oz (225 g) red or yellow pepper, de-seeded and sliced
2 tablespoons oil
2 teaspoons fresh root ginger, grated
2 tablespoons soy sauce
2 tablespoons medium sherry

First prepare all the vegetables. Heat the oil until very hot and fry the root ginger for a few seconds. Then add the onions and fry for 2 minutes. Now add the remaining vegetables and cook these, still over a high heat, for 3–4 minutes, stirring constantly. Mix together the soy sauce and sherry and pour these over the vegetables. Cook for a further 2 minutes and serve straight away.

Salads and DRESSINGS

Mixed Green Salad ❧ Summer Salad ❧ Classic Tomato Salad
Oriental Rice Salad ❧ Greek Salad with Feta ❧ Flemish Salad
Rice Salad with Herbs ❧ Tabbouleh ❧ Coleslaw
Cheese and Fennel Coleslaw ❧ Apple, Carrot and Sunflower Seed Coleslaw
Red Cabbage Coleslaw ❧ Marinaded Bean Salads
Portuguese Bean Salad ❧ Salad Quebec ❧ Greek Bean Salad
Prickley Green Beetroot Salad ❧ Vinaigrette Dressing ❧ Mayonnaise
Blue Cheese Dressing ❧ Honey and Lemon Dressing
Summer Salad Dressing ❧ Oriental Dressing ❧ Tofu Dressing
Savoury Tofu Dressing

I've always enjoyed eating vegetables raw for their fresh colour and crunchy texture. With a little thought it is possible to make interesting and unusual salads all the year round. In this section you'll find recipes for a variety of summer and winter salads which can accompany a wide range of main courses or make a light meal on their own.

Beans and grains can also provide the basis for salads so I've included a delicious Greek Bean Salad recipe where haricot beans are cooked in a tasty tomato sauce, and my version of Tabbouleh, which is the traditional wheat salad from the Middle East. It has a marvellous herb dressing. In contrast to these, the Oriental Rice Salad is a tasty mixture of bean sprouts and rice.

Even the most basic salad can be transformed by a good dressing. Apart from those standbys, mayonnaise and vinaigrette, why not try out something a little more adventurous such as Blue Cheese Dressing or even Tofu Dressing which is unusual and delicious.

MIXED GREEN SALAD

Green salads can be a meal in themselves once you think beyond the lettuce leaf. The range of greenery available is enormous from the dark shades of watercress to the pale hue of spring onions. It's worth making salads a feature of a meal rather than an afterthought.

Serves 4
1 small lettuce
1 bunch spring onions, cleaned and finely chopped
4 sticks celery, trimmed and chopped
$\frac{1}{2}$ cucumber, washed and sliced into rings
1 avocado, peeled and cut into chunks
1 bunch watercress, cleaned
1 quantity of Vinaigrette Dressing (page 201)

First prepare the lettuce by separating out the leaves and wiping them with a damp cloth. Then prepare all the other vegetables, put all the ingredients into a large salad bowl and moisten with the vinaigrette. It is best to toss green salads with your hands as this prevents the fragile leaves from becoming bruised.

SUMMER SALAD

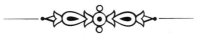

Raw food plays an important part in a diet not only for vegetarians but also for everyone interested in healthy eating. Salads are an excellent way of providing essential vitamins and minerals which might otherwise be lost in the cooking process. I often make several salads to complement a meal, but a single salad made of root vegetables, fruits and leafy vegetables contains a good range of essential nutrients. (I remember this rule by the rhyming words – root, shoot and fruit.) In the 1920s Doctor Bircher-Benner, who invented muesli, developed this idea as he believed raw foods to be an essential part of a healthy diet. He had much success in treating patients using a mainly raw food diet. This one is just a simple starting point.

Serves 4
1 small lettuce, washed
1 medium carrot, scrubbed and grated
3–4 sticks celery, trimmed and sliced
⅓ cucumber, diced
1 apple, washed, cored and diced
1 small onion, peeled and finely chopped
1 lb (450 g) tomatoes, washed and sliced
mustard and cress
1 quantity of Vinaigrette Dressing (page 201)

Prepare all the ingredients and put them into a large salad bowl. Mix them straight away with the dressing as this coating of oil and vinegar prevents some of the vitamins and minerals from being destroyed by contact with the air. I think it is better to mix in a dressing by hand as you are less likely to bruise any delicate ingredients. Serve the salad chilled.

CLASSIC TOMATO SALAD

This simple way of serving tomatoes is one of my summer favourites. The salt, pepper and sugar mixture draws out juices from the tomatoes so that they create their own dressing. Serve this as a side salad, garnished with watercress.

Serves 4
1 lb (450 g) tomatoes, sliced
1½ teaspoons salt
½ teaspoon freshly ground black pepper
½ teaspoon demerara sugar
a little cider vinegar if required

Garnish:
1 bunch watercress

Slice the tomatoes and lay them on a plate. Mix together the salt, pepper and sugar and sprinkle this mixture over the tomatoes. Leave them to stand, preferably in the refrigerator or a cool place, for 15 minutes. Put them into a serving dish lined with watercress, and sprinkle on a little extra vinegar if you like a sharper flavour.

ORIENTAL RICE SALAD

This is a delicious savoury salad which could be a meal in itself, especially if you add some of the optional extras. The dressing has an oriental flavour with its fruit base flavoured with ginger and soy sauce. For a variation on this theme I like to mix other cooked grains with the rice, such as wheat or barley, as they provide a contrast in colour and texture. This makes a good accompaniment to flans or other savoury dishes.

Serves 4

8 oz (225 g) long-grain brown rice, washed
18 fl oz (525 ml) water
salt and freshly ground black pepper

For the dressing:
2 tablespoons fresh orange juice
2 tablespoons oil, preferably sunflower
1 dessertspoon soy sauce
1 clove garlic, crushed
½ teaspoon root ginger, freshly grated
1 dessertspoon sherry (optional)
salt and freshly ground black pepper

For the salad ingredients:
6 radishes, cleaned and sliced
2 oz (50 g) fresh bean sprouts
2 oz (50 g) raisins
1 orange, peeled and segmented

Optional extras:
2 oz (50 g) lightly toasted cashew nuts
2 sticks celery, trimmed and diced
4 oz (110 g) fresh pineapple, cubed

Bring the water to the boil and when it is boiling add the rice. Stir once, turn the heat down and simmer with the pan covered for 25–30 minutes or until the rice is cooked. Then season lightly with salt and freshly ground black pepper.

Meanwhile prepare the dressing by mixing all the ingredients together in a screw-top jar. Shake them vigorously so that the flavours blend. Pour the dressing over the rice while it is still warm as it will then absorb more flavour. Prepare the salad ingredients and when the rice is cool mix everything together, pile it into a serving dish and serve.

GREEK SALAD WITH FETA

This is a lovely variation on the Classic Tomato Salad (page 186), as the seasonings go well with the strong taste of goat's cheese. This recipe can become a full meal when served with crusty rolls, celery sticks and Greek Bean Salad (page 199), or you can simply use it as a side salad piled on top of a bed of lettuce or endive.

Serves 4–6

12 oz (350 g) feta cheese or similar goat's cheese
freshly ground black pepper
2 tablespoons olive oil
1 tablespoon white wine vinegar
1 quantity of Classic Tomato Salad (page 186)
2 oz (50 g) green, stuffed olives
1 bunch spring onions, finely chopped
1 teaspoon fennel seed (optional)

Cut the cheese into cubes, put them into a bowl and grind some black pepper over the top. Mix together the oil and vinegar and pour this over the cheese. Chill for at least 30 minutes. Arrange the tomato salad in a serving dish and pile the marinaded goat's cheese over the top. Sprinkle with stuffed olives, finely chopped spring onions and fennel seed.

FLEMISH SALAD

The beautifully shaped leaves and colour of chicory are the basis for this classic salad. Choose heads of chicory that are mainly white in colour to get the best flavour. Both from the nutritional and visual points of view, it is best to leave the chicory blades whole. If you cut them, they will soon discolour.

Serves 4
1 head chicory
2 oranges
6 sticks celery
1 bunch watercress
1 quantity of Blue Cheese Dressing (page 203)

Separate the blades of chicory but leave them whole. Peel and segment the oranges and cut them into small pieces. Trim the celery, clean it and cut it on the diagonal. Then mix the ingredients together and pour over the dressing. Alternatively lay out a bed of watercress and arrange the chicory blades on it like the petals of a flower. Cover these with slices of orange in a circular pattern and pile the chopped celery into the centre. Then hand the dressing around separately.

RICE SALAD WITH HERBS

This is a simple dish where the rice is marinaded in a vinaigrette dressing and then flavoured with fresh herbs. It is good with many different savouries or flans.

Serves 4
8 oz (225 g) brown rice, washed
18 fl oz (525 ml) water
4 tablespoons oil
2 tablespoons white wine or cider vinegar
1 clove garlic, crushed
salt and freshly ground black pepper
1–2 tablespoons fresh parsley, finely chopped
1–2 tablespoons fresh chives, finely chopped

Bring the water to the boil and add the rice, stirring once. Cover the pan and cook gently for 25–30 minutes or until the rice is soft and the water has been absorbed. Mix together the oil, vinegar, garlic, salt and black pepper and stir this dressing into the rice while it is still warm so that the rice soaks up all the flavour as it cools. When the rice is cool mix in the parsley and chives. Alternatively you could add other fresh green herbs, such as basil, or spring onions.

TABBOULEH

I've eaten many variations of this traditional Middle Eastern salad; my favourite is heavily laced with garlic and herbs. A key ingredient is bulgar or burghul wheat. This is a partially cooked cracked wheat, similar to couscous, and it only needs soaking for a short while before it is ready to eat (see page 139). Bulgar wheat makes a delicious salad base as it is so light in texture. Some people even mistake it for white rice!

In this recipe, which is my personal version of Tabbouleh, the bulgar wheat is marinaded in dressing overnight so that the flavours soak in. The tomatoes and cucumber are then added the next day. I use rather less parsley than you would find in the Lebanese version but add more if you prefer. Tabbouleh goes well with flans, cold pies and roasts.

Serves 6
7 oz (175–200 g) bulgar wheat
1 teaspoon salt
12 fl oz (330 ml) boiling water
For the dressing:
2 fl oz (50 ml) olive oil
2fl oz (50 ml) lemon juice
2 tablespoons fresh mint, finely chopped
1–2 cloves garlic, crushed
6 tablespoons fresh parsley, finely chopped
1 lb (450 g) tomatoes, chopped
½ cucumber, diced

Mix the bulgar wheat with the salt, pour over the boiling water and leave it for 15–20 minutes. The wheat will swell and absorb the water. (You can use cold water but I find using boiling water works much more quickly.) Mix the dressing ingredients together and pour the mixture over the soaked bulgar, then leave it overnight in a refrigerator or cool place. Next day, fold in the salad ingredients and serve.

COLESLAW

I well remember the first time I ate coleslaw and really enjoyed it as a salad – just a simple combination of carrots and white cabbage with apples and raisins added, coated in mayonnaise. I believed at the time it was the only coleslaw possible and I only realised later that there were endless variations possible with different vegetables, fruits and nuts. I began experimenting and making more and more extravagant, colourful salads that seemed to have less cabbage and more of everything else! But although it is fun to use lots of different ingredients, simple combinations are often the most effective and the least work. Bearing that in mind, here are some simple variations on the basic cabbage slaw.

CHEESE AND FENNEL COLESLAW

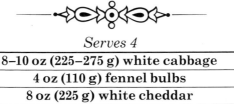

Serves 4
8–10 oz (225–275 g) white cabbage
4 oz (110 g) fennel bulbs
8 oz (225 g) white cheddar
$\frac{1}{4}$ pint (150 ml) natural yoghurt or mayonnaise
fennel tops to garnish

Wash the cabbage and the fennel and remove any hard outside leaves and the central core if it is too tough. Then shred them finely, cutting along the direction of the growth. Put the shredded vegetables into a large bowl and grate in the cheese. Mix them all together thoroughly, then spoon in the yoghurt or mayonnaise and toss so that all the ingredients are well coated. Place the salad in its serving dish and, using a pair of scissors, snip the fennel tops over the top. Serve chilled.

APPLE, CARROT AND SUNFLOWER SEED COLESLAW

Serves 4
1 tablespoon sunflower seeds
1 tablespoon concentrated apple juice or orange juice
8–10 oz (225–275 g) white cabbage
2 dessert apples
6 oz (175 g) carrots, peeled
1 tablespoon oil (preferably sunflower oil)
1 tablespoon cider vinegar or white wine vinegar
1 teaspoon honey
1 heaped teaspoon fresh (chopped) basil or ½ teaspoon dried basil

Soak the sunflower seeds in the concentrated apple or orange juice for 30 minutes to 1 hour so that they swell up. Wash and finely shred the cabbage, removing the hard outside leaves and the centre stalk if it is too tough, and pat dry.

In a large bowl mix together the oil, vinegar, honey and basil, then add the cabbage and toss so that it becomes well coated. Grate the apples and carrot over the top and toss again. Finally, add the soaked sunflower seeds, reserving a few to sprinkle on the top. Transfer the coleslaw to a serving dish, sprinkle on the remaining sunflower seeds and serve chilled.

RED CABBAGE COLESLAW

Serves 4

8–10 oz (225–275 g) red cabbage
4 oz (110 g) black grapes
8 radishes, washed and sliced
4 oz (110 g) walnuts
4 tablespoons Vinaigrette Dressing (page 201)

Wash and finely shred the cabbage, removing any tough outside leaves and the central core. Pat dry and place in a large bowl. Wash the grapes, slice them in half and remove the seeds. Wash and slice the radishes and chop the walnuts roughly. Mix these ingredients together with the red cabbage and then toss everything in the vinaigrette. Put the salad into a large serving bowl and chill.

MARINADED BEAN SALADS

In its simplest form a bean salad can be a mixture of salad ingredients with just one type of cooked bean. The addition of beans gives texture and substance to a salad if it is to be more than a light side dish. Mixed bean salads take longer to prepare as each type of bean needs to be cooked separately to keep a good colour, but for a party it looks wonderful and is very much worth the effort. I tend to stick to a combination of two beans, picking contrasting colours.

I've suggested a choice of two marinades. One is dark and spicy, which is more suitable for red kidney beans or black-eyed beans, and the other is light and sharp and more suitable for flageolet beans, butter beans or chick peas. The flavour and look of beans improves immensely when they are marinaded, especially if this is done when the beans are still warm. Immediately they are cooked, soak them in the marinade and as they cool they will soak up the flavours of the dressing. The remaining liquid can then be drained away and used as a flavouring for a soup or casserole. The marinaded beans will keep for three or four days in the refrigerator.

DARK AND SPICY MARINADE

6 fl oz (175 ml) olive oil
3 fl oz (75 ml) red wine vinegar
½ teaspoon salt
½ teaspoon freshly ground coriander
1 teaspoon ground cumin
½ teaspoon chilli powder
1 clove garlic, crushed

Mix all the ingredients together thoroughly and pour them over the freshly cooked, drained beans. Let the beans cool in the liquid and then drain away any excess dressing before serving.

LIGHT AND SHARP MARINADE

6 fl oz (175 ml) oil (preferably sunflower oil)
3 fl oz (75 ml) lemon juice
½ teaspoon salt
freshly ground black pepper
½ teaspoon dry mustard
½ teaspoon freshly grated root ginger
1 clove garlic, crushed

Mix all the ingredients together thoroughly and pour them over freshly cooked beans. Let the beans cool in the liquid and then drain away any excess marinade before using the beans for a salad.

Here are two easy bean salads which are completely contrasting in colour and texture. I've given quantities which would be suitable for a party as I find these salads are always popular and go a long way.

PORTUGUESE BEAN SALAD

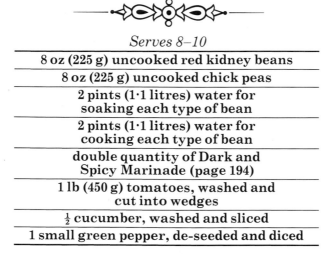

Serves 8–10

8 oz (225 g) uncooked red kidney beans
8 oz (225 g) uncooked chick peas
2 pints (1·1 litres) water for soaking each type of bean
2 pints (1·1 litres) water for cooking each type of bean
double quantity of Dark and Spicy Marinade (page 194)
1 lb (450 g) tomatoes, washed and cut into wedges
½ cucumber, washed and sliced
1 small green pepper, de-seeded and diced

First prepare the 2 types of pulses by soaking them in separate bowls of water overnight. The next day, drain away the water and bring the beans to the boil in fresh water in separate pans. (If dark beans are cooked with pale-coloured beans they all end up the same colour, so it's important to cook them separately.) Boil both pots of beans fast for 10 minutes and then turn the heat down to a simmer. Cover the pan and continue cooking until the beans are tender. With red kidney beans this takes about 40 minutes. With chick peas it can take between 40 minutes to 90 minutes depending on the age of the chick peas.

When the beans are tender enough to bite through, drain away the cooking liquid, or keep it for a soup or stock. Then put the beans

195

together in a large bowl and pour over the marinade. Let the beans cool completely in the marinade and if you have too much liquid, spoon some off.

Prepare the salad ingredients and when the beans are completely cold, mix both together, moistening with a little of the excess marinade if necessary. Chill before serving.

SALAD QUEBEC

Serves 8–10

8 oz (225 g) uncooked flageolet beans
2 pints (1·1 litres) water for soaking
2 pints (1·1 litres) water for cooking
1 quantity of Light and Sharp Marinade (page 194)
12 oz (350 g) cabbage, finely shredded
6 oz (175 g) carrots, scrubbed and grated
1 small green pepper, de-seeded and cut into thin strips

First prepare the beans by soaking them overnight in the water. Next day, drain them and bring to the boil in fresh water. Boil fast for 10 minutes, then turn the heat down to a simmer and continue cooking until the beans are just tender. With flageolet beans and other white beans this takes between 30–35 minutes. When they are cooked, drain away the cooking liquid, reserving it for a soup or stock. Put the beans in a large bowl and soak them in the marinade. Let the beans cool completely, then drain the excess marinade away. Prepare the salad ingredients, mix them with the marinaded beans and moisten with a little extra marinade if you think it necessary. Chill before serving.

OPPOSITE:
Red Dragon Pie (*page 125*)
Chilli Bean Casserole (*page 126*)
Spiced Chick Peas (*page 127*)
Lentil Croquettes (*page 130*)

GREEK BEAN SALAD

This is a colourful dish, ideal to accompany a quiche or savoury roast. It is also delicious eaten with fresh bread, pickles and cheese for a variation on the standard ploughman's lunch.

Serves 4–6

8 oz (225 g) haricot beans
2 pints (1·1 litres) water for soaking
2 pints (1·1 litres) water for boiling
3 fl oz (75 ml) olive oil
1 bay leaf
1 teaspoon dried thyme
1 teaspoon dried oregano
2 tablespoons tomato purée
salt and freshly ground black pepper
juice of ½ lemon
1 bunch spring onions, chopped
1 red or green pepper, de-seeded and diced

Garnish:
slices of lemon
black olives
1 hard-boiled egg, sliced

Soak the beans overnight. Next day, drain and rinse them, then bring to the boil in fresh water. Boil fast for 10 minutes, skimming off any scum which forms on the surface. Reduce the heat and simmer in a covered pan for about 30 minutes, then drain and allow to cool.

Heat the olive oil in a saucepan and fry the beans with herbs gently for 10 minutes. Add enough water to cover the beans by 1 inch (2·5 cm) and stir in 2 tablespoons of tomato purée. Simmer gently, uncovered, for 45 minutes. The liquid will have reduced to leave a thick tomato covering on the beans. Let this cool, then season well and add the lemon juice. Add the salad vegetables and transfer to an attractive serving dish and garnish.

OPPOSITE:
Broccoli in Lemon Cream Sauce (*page 165*)
Stuffed Courgettes (*page 168*)
Paprika Potatoes (*page 175*)

PRICKLEY GREEN BEETROOT SALAD

Actress Kate O'Mara has been a vegetarian for 20 years. Although she eats eggs and cheese she is fondest of raw vegetables and salads. This recipe is one of her favourite salads and is ideal for a quick and easy lunch. It goes well with some fresh wholemeal bread. Prickley Green Beetroot Salad is originally the idea of a friend of Kate's and the name derives from the village where she lives — Prickley Green, Worcestershire.

Kate prefers her beetroot to be raw, but you can cook it first if you prefer.

Serves 4
2 large raw beetroot, grated
1 large onion, chopped
4 oz (110 g) sultanas
2 tablespoons oil (preferably sunflower oil)
$\frac{1}{2}$ teaspoon dried basil
salt and freshly ground pepper
juice of 1 lemon
Garnish:
1 bunch spring onions, chopped

Mix all the ingredients together in a salad bowl. Sprinkle the spring onions over the top and serve.

VINAIGRETTE DRESSING

There are no hard and fast rules about vinaigrette dressing but the most common ratio is three parts olive oil to one of vinegar. It depends entirely on your personal preference and the type of salad that you want to dress whether you choose a sharp or creamy flavour. The oil can be either olive oil or sunflower oil and the vinegar can be wine, herb or cider vinegar or lemon juice. I particularly like my spicy version, given here, for green salad.

1 tablespoon vinegar, preferably cider
pinch each of mustard powder, horseradish and paprika
3 tablespoons oil, preferably olive oil

Put the vinegar in a screw-top jar and add the mustard powder, horseradish and paprika. Shake this thoroughly. When the spices are blended add the olive oil and shake again until all the ingredients have combined. This can then be used straight away or kept for a short while in the refrigerator. Always shake thoroughly before using.

MAYONNAISE

It is well worth making your own mayonnaise. It does not take long to do and you can obtain the exact flavour and consistency you like. I make mayonnaise using an electric whisk as I find I can control the consistency more easily than by any other method. The most important thing to remember is to drip the oil in *literally drop by drop*. This way the egg yolks should not curdle. In some European countries you can buy special spouted jugs to do this but if you cannot get one of these I've found the best method is to use a fork. Dip it into a jug of oil then shake off the droplets into the egg yolks as you beat. It is then easy to build up a steady rhythm and you are sure not to put in too much oil at once.

The oil for mayonnaise can either be all olive oil, or a mixture of olive oil and sunflower oil if you prefer a lighter consistency. I've also suggested some variations.

Makes ½ pint (275 ml) mayonnaise
2 egg yolks
½ pint (275 ml) olive oil or mixed oils
2 tablespoons white wine vinegar or lemon juice and vinegar
salt and freshly ground black pepper

Beat the egg yolks thoroughly in a small bowl. Then add the olive oil drop by drop. Do this by dipping a fork into the oil and then shaking droplets into the beaten egg yolks. Beat this mixture constantly with an electric whisk. When about half the oil has been added, the mixture will be very thick. Add 1 tablespoon of the vinegar to thin this down and then add the rest of the oil, pouring it in in a steady stream. Thin down the mayonnaise with the remaining vinegar to taste and then season it with salt and pepper. Should the eggs curdle, beat up another egg yolk in a fresh bowl and then add the curdled mayonnaise to it very gradually, beating all the time. If your mayonnaise is still too thick at the end of the process thin it with a little boiling water.

AIOLI
This is the traditional mayonnaise from Provence which is a richer version because it contains extra egg yolk. It is also highly flavoured with garlic. Make it in exactly the same way as in the previous recipe but begin by beating together 3 egg yolks with 3 cloves of crushed garlic.

MAYONNAISE CREAM
Combine equal parts of mayonnaise with yoghurt or sour cream and mix them thoroughly. This makes a lighter dressing for a coleslaw.

SPICED MAYONNAISE
Add ½ teaspoon of either curry powder, mustard powder, cayenne pepper or paprika to the finished mayonnaise and allow the mixture to stand for ½ hour before using.

BLUE CHEESE DRESSING

This is a delicious dressing with a creamy texture and strong flavour. No salt is necessary because the cheese already contains plenty. It is a useful variation on mayonnaise to serve with coleslaws and is lovely with Flemish Salad (page 188). I use it as a dip for crudités as well. It keeps 2–3 days in the refrigerator in a screw-top jar.

Makes ⅓ pint (180 ml) dressing
1 egg yolk
¼ pint (150 ml) oil (preferably sunflower oil)
1–2 tablespoons lemon juice
2 oz (50 g) blue cheese
2 tablespoons soured cream or yoghurt
1 heaped teaspoon dill, chopped
1 clove garlic, crushed
freshly ground black pepper

First make a mayonnaise by beating the egg yolk and adding the oil drop by drop, beating thoroughly. It is easiest to do this with an electric whisk. When half the oil is added, mix in 1 tablespoon of lemon juice. Then add the remaining oil, 1 tablespoon at a time, beating thoroughly. Add the remaining lemon juice. Crumble or mash in the blue cheese and then stir in the soured cream or yoghurt, dill and garlic. Season with plenty of freshly ground black pepper.

HONEY AND LEMON DRESSING

This is a sweet and light dressing that makes a refreshing change from vinaigrette. It is suitable for most green salads, coleslaws or fruit salads.

Makes ½ pint (275 ml) dressing
6 fl oz (175 ml) oil (preferably sunflower oil)
2 fl oz (55 ml) lemon juice
2 fl oz (55 ml) clear honey
1 teaspoon grated onion
¼ teaspoon mustard powder
1 teaspoon sweet paprika
1 teaspoon celery seed

Combine all the ingredients in a bowl and whisk thoroughly. Allow this to stand for 15 minutes, then whisk again before using.

SUMMER SALAD DRESSING

This is a creamy dressing made from blended yoghurt and cottage cheese so it is low in calories. The ingredients should be combined in a liquidiser so that they blend well together into a deliciously light cream. This makes a refreshing contrast from mayonnaise as a coleslaw dressing or salad dip.

Makes ½ pint (275 ml) dressing
5 oz (150 g) cottage cheese
¼ pint (150 ml) natural yoghurt
1 tablespoon mayonnaise
1 dessertspoon lemon juice
1 dessertspoon olive oil
salt and freshly ground black pepper to taste
Garnish:
freshly snipped chives

Put all the ingredients into a liquidiser and blend thoroughly for about 30 seconds. Then pour the dressing into a bowl or jug and season to taste. Toss your salad in it or serve separately in a bowl garnished with freshly snipped chives as a dressing or dip.

ORIENTAL DRESSING

Soy sauce, vinegar, tofu and honey are the most common ingredients in Japanese salad dressing, but I have made an East–West adaptation of the traditional version using a dark vinaigrette highlighted with oriental seasoning. In contrast to the light vinaigrette dressings which help to enhance the crispy quality of green salad, this dressing is rich and more suitable for rice or for cooked or soft vegetables which benefit from marinading.

Makes ⅓ pint (180 ml) dressing
6 tablespoons oil (preferably a mixture of olive and sunflower oils)
2 teaspoons red wine vinegar
4 teaspoons soy sauce
½ teaspoon root ginger, freshly grated
1 tablespoon sherry

Put everything together in a large screw-top jar and shake vigorously until the ingredients are emulsified. Serve straight away with a rice or bulgar wheat salad, cooked beans or stir-fry vegetables.

TOFU DRESSING

Tofu (pronounced toe-foo) is a relatively new food to us but has been a staple part of the oriental diet for years. It is actually a soya bean curd. Tofu may well lead to a food revolution here as it is low in calories and fats, free from cholesterol and is fairly cheap. It has reached us from China and Japan via America and is becoming increasingly available in this country.

There are several different types. First there is firm tofu available from oriental supermarkets. This has been pressed and is useful for deep-frying and stir-frying. Then there are tofu burgers which are spicy combinations of vegetables. The most common form, however, is Silken Tofu which is a pure white substance sold in a sealed carton and has the consistency of solid cream. This type is available in most health food stores and wholefood shops. Although it can be dried out by pressing it or by wrapping it tightly in a cloth, this type is best used as it is for making into creams, dips and sauces and is absolutely delicious. The simple dressing given below has a creamy consistency with a fresh lemon tang and can be used in place of mayonnaise, yoghurt or sour cream dressings.

$1 \times 10\frac{1}{2}$ oz (297 g) packet Silken Tofu
2 tablespoons fresh lemon juice
2 tablespoons oil (preferably sunflower oil)
1 clove garlic, crushed

Put all the ingredients into a liquidiser and blend until smooth. Use as required.

SAVOURY TOFU DRESSING

Tofu is very sensitive to other flavours. The addition of just a little soy sauce transforms plain Tofu Dressing into an ideal sauce for croquettes and roasts.

1 quantity of Tofu Dressing (above)
1 teaspoon soy sauce

Put the ingredients into a liquidiser and blend until smooth. Use as required.

Breads and BISCUITS

Wholewheat Bread Dough ❧ Pizza ❧ Sesame Sablés
Brazilian Croustade ❧ Vegetable Croustade ❧ Wholewheat Scones
Rich Bread Ring ❧ Corn Bread Muffins

Wholewheat bread is one of the staples of a vegetarian diet but it has also become extremely popular with non-vegetarians in recent years. Not only does it have lots more flavour than white bread, but it keeps better and is a valuable source of dietary fibre. In this chapter I've described how to make a wholewheat dough which can be used for loaves, rolls or pizzas. If you haven't tried using wholewheat flour before you'll find it very easy and the superior taste of wholewheat bread ample reward for your efforts.

I always make my breadcrumbs from wholewheat bread too; the taste is very much better than the bought variety. They can be used in exactly the same way as white breadcrumbs, for thickening a nut roast, coating a croquette, or making a savoury pie base, called a croustade. If you use a liquidiser or food processor they can be made very quickly and they also freeze well. In the chapter on Puddings (page 223) there is a recipe for a delicious ice-cream using wholewheat breadcrumbs.

Bread need not only be made from wholewheat flour, of course, and I've included one of my favourite recipes for a rich bread dough which is made from strong white flour and used to make a spectacular savoury bread ring. In addition, there is a recipe for Corn Bread Muffins which are made with a mixture of corn meal and wholewheat flour.

WHOLEWHEAT BREAD

My grandfather was a miller and owned his own mill in Sussex. At first it was driven by an engine but after he'd been there a short while he restored the old water wheel, and so it became a water mill. He had two millers — Slee and Puttock. Puttock could frequently be seen sitting on sacks in the lane stone dressing, which is a highly skilled job. To dress a stone means to re-cut the grooves in it which wear down after about 100 hours of milling. The dressing of a stone could take Puttock up to 18 hours.

My grandfather was proud of his flour, describing it as 'Pure, unbleached, untreated, unadulterated stone-ground flour' and he used to pack up 7 lb bags and send them all round the country. His wholemeal flour made beautiful bread. Strange how life comes full circle, since I now bake over 300 loaves a week.

There are endless ways of making bread and somehow a great mystique has grown up about it. It is actually very simple to do and I think the nature of both the flour and yeast we use today has greatly improved, giving us a much greater chance of success. Many people don't make bread because they think it will be time-consuming, but the basic procedure is very quick. Dough can be frozen uncooked, so it's simple to make a large batch and only bake each loaf as you need it. The basic ingredients are flour, yeast, salt and water.

FLOUR

Wholewheat flour
Wholewheat or wholemeal flours (they are the same thing) contain the whole of the product derived from milling wheat. Wholewheat flours vary from brand to brand, so it's worth trying several varieties until you find one to suit you. I try to buy a stone-ground flour which means that the wheatgerm oil is evenly distributed through the flour; the texture of this type of flour will vary according to the gap between the two grinding stones. I also prefer a strong or hard flour for bread-making because that contains more gluten than soft flour and so will rise more easily and have a lighter texture.

Wheatmeal flour
It's easy to confuse wholemeal or wholewheat flour with wheatmeal. Wheatmeal flour has been milled in such a way as to remove some of the bran – up to 20% in fact. It is a lighter flour with a paler colour and although it isn't quite as nutritious as wholemeal, it is very suitable for making cakes.

YEAST

The amount of yeast you use will depend on the length of time you are prepared to let the dough rise. Both the flavour and texture of the baked bread will vary according to how long you leave the dough. If you leave it overnight, for example, the bread can taste very beery, because given time, moisture and warmth, the flour undergoes a kind of natural fermentation. Sometimes this explains why bread made with too much yeast in it has a rather sour or acid flavour.

Remember that dried yeast is twice as strong as fresh yeast, so use about half the quantity of dried to fresh. (A teaspoon of dried yeast is about $\frac{1}{2}$ oz (10 g).) Dried yeast which has been kept too long on the shelf goes stale and is therefore useless. Always buy your yeast from a shop with a quick turnover and do not keep it too long in your cupboard. If dried yeast does not froth up when mixed with water it is 'dead'; throw it away and start again with a new packet of yeast.

A wholewheat loaf will never rise as high as a white loaf because wholewheat flour contains less gluten in it than white flour which stops the yeast working quite so well, but as real brown bread is so much more delicious, this does not seem to me to be a disadvantage.

SALT

Salt strengthens the gluten in the flour and so helps the rising action. It also brings out the flavour of the grain and regulates the yeast. By the way, never put salted water straight on to yeast or you will kill it. Bread without salt has a very different texture and, I think, not so good a flavour. Experiment to see how much you prefer and, whatever you do, make sure the salt is carefully and evenly distributed throughout the flour before you start making the bread.

WATER

Wholewheat flour needs more water than white flour because of its extra bran content. I find it's better to have a slightly wet dough because it seems to be easier to work with and gives you a better texture at the end. If your bread is brick-like this is possibly because you didn't put enough water in the dough. When I've taught children to make bread, I've found they often don't like the initial stickiness of the dough and have added a lot more flour to counteract it. Then they find they've dried out the dough too much and the end result is very hard. The water needs to be warm, preferably 80–95 °F (30–35 °C). You will achieve about the right temperature if you use one-third boiling water to two-thirds cold water. Yeast cells will grow at a lower temperature but very slowly, so the rising will take longer.

These four ingredients then make you a very good basic loaf, but there are a number of things you can add to vary the texture and taste of your bread.

SUGAR

Sugar is usually added to bread in the belief that it is a food for the yeast but in fact the modern compressed yeasts don't need it. From the minute the yeast comes into contact with a tepid liquid it starts coming back to life and adding sugar often dissipates some of the carbon dioxide which might otherwise be raising the flour. However, sugar is needed when making sweet loaves and I often put a little molasses in my bread dough, simply because I think it adds to the flavour.

BUTTER OR OIL

Adding butter or oil will give your dough a more springy texture. Oil in particular makes the dough easier to knead and will often stop a crust forming when you leave the dough to prove. Too much will inhibit the growth of the yeast, however, so if you want a very rich buttery dough let the yeast work through the flour first, and add the butter afterwards.

EGGS

Adding eggs helps to bind the dough and gives it a more cake-like flavour, although too many eggs will sometimes dry it out.

Of course there is a whole range of dried fruits, nuts and spices which you can also add to make your bread more special, particularly for a festive occasion.

WHOLEWHEAT BREAD DOUGH

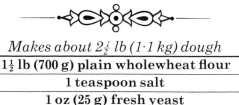

Makes about 2½ lb (1·1 kg) dough

1½ lb (700 g) plain wholewheat flour
1 teaspoon salt
1 oz (25 g) fresh yeast
1 teaspoon molasses or 1 dessertspoon brown sugar
¾ pint (400 ml) water (⅔ cold, ⅓ boiling)
1 tablespoon oil

Pre-heat the oven to gas mark 7, 425°F (220°C).

Mix the yeast and molasses together and pour in ¼ pint (150 ml) water. Beat vigorously until the yeast has dissolved. Leave in a warm place for 5 minutes or until the surface is frothy. Put the flour into a bowl with the salt and mix well. Then pour the yeast mixture over the flour, add the oil and the rest of the water and stir with a wooden spoon.

As the dough forms, start to knead it, then tip it out onto a surface and knead well, either 100 times or for about 10 minutes. A food processor will take the hard work out of kneading by producing well kneaded dough in 1 minute. Put the dough into a clean bowl and cover with a damp cloth. Leave it somewhere warm until it has doubled in size. This takes about an hour.

Next tip the dough out of the bowl and knock it down by punching your fist into the middle so that all the gas is knocked out. Then knead it again for about 10 minutes.

If you are baking loaves, weigh the dough into 1 lb (450 g) pieces, knead them into shape and put them into greased loaf tins. If you are making rolls weigh the dough into 3 oz (75 g) sections and shape them into rounds or crescents and place them on a greased baking sheet.

Leave the dough to rise again for about 20 to 30 minutes then bake in a hot oven. Loaves take 35–40 minutes and rolls take 15–20 minutes. Test a finished loaf by tapping its base. If it has been baked long enough it should sound hollow. This can be quite tricky to judge, but you will soon learn to distinguish the right sound. If you feel you've taken it out too soon, it is quite all right to put it back in the oven for another few minutes without its tin.

Cool the loaves or rolls on a rack as soon as they leave the oven, because this prevents any steam trapped in the tin from making the base of the bread soggy. Bread is delicious hot from the oven, but don't eat it too hot or you will get dreadful indigestion!

GLAZING AND DECORATING

A glaze on a loaf looks attractive and is easy to do. Apply an egg glaze – made from a beaten egg with a little added salt – after the dough has risen. This will give the bread a good crust. A sugar or honey glaze can be put on after the bread is baked to add a shine to a finished loaf.

Seeds and grains make interesting toppings on bread. You can use poppy seeds, caraway, aniseed, sesame or sunflower seeds, as well as cracked wheat and buckwheat.

FREEZING

All types of bread can be frozen either as whole loaves or ready-sliced. Use air-tight containers so that the bread won't be affected by other foods in the freezer. Uncooked dough can also be frozen, but let it thaw properly and prove before baking.

WHAT TO LOOK FOR IF THINGS GO WRONG

Wet and heavy bread sometimes means that you have let it rise too long and the dough has collapsed. There is a difference between the dough rising and forming a rounded shape or reaching a limit when it seems to flatten off. If you put it in the oven when it has flattened off, it sinks in on itself. It's just a matter of learning through experience.

When you get holes in the bread either in the centre or at the top, you have either not been firm enough with your kneading or you have not kneaded for long enough.

If the end result is very dense, this can mean you haven't kneaded the dough sufficiently or that you have not left it to rise long enough. Try to be a bit more patient!

If the bread bakes unevenly or lop-sidedly, the oven heat is not properly distributed. Turn the loaf round while baking it or change its position in the oven.

Don't let all this put you off, however. Even if you do make a few mistakes to start with, wholewheat bread tastes delicious, is very good for you since it is full of fibre and has an irresistible smell while it is baking, so do have a go.

PIZZA

There is plenty of scope for variety with pizzas. They make excellent supper and lunch dishes and toppings can be devised to suit any occasion. Wholewheat pizza is fairly filling and to be confronted with a whole one can be rather daunting so I usually make a large one and then serve it in slices.

In order to avoid the base becoming soggy it is a good idea to bake it first so that it crisps up, then add the topping and return the pizza to the oven to finish cooking. Uncooked dough can be frozen either in blocks or ready rolled out into bases. Pizza can also be frozen complete with the topping in place, but do not add the cheese until you are actually ready to bake the pizza.

The following recipe is for a basic pizza but there are many different combinations of vegetables which could be used for the topping. Pizzas are delicious on their own or accompanied by salads.

Serves 4–6
13 oz (375 g) wholewheat dough (i.e. $\frac{1}{3}$ of recipe on page 211)
1 tablespoon oil
$\frac{1}{2}$ lb (225 g) onions, peeled and finely chopped
1–2 cloves garlic, crushed
1–2 tablespoons tomato purée
1 × 14 oz (400 g) tin of tomatoes
1 teaspoon dried basil
1 teaspoon dried oregano
salt and freshly ground pepper
6 oz (175 g) grated cheese (Cheddar is fine but mozzarella is more authentic

Suggestions for garnish:
black and green olives
tomatoes, thickly sliced
green peppercorns
capers
red and green peppers, diced

Pre-heat the oven to gas mark 7, 425°F (220°C).

Roll out the dough in a large round, 12 inches (30 cm) in diameter or a rectangle 11 × 7 inches (28 × 18 cm). Prick it all over so that it rises evenly. Leave it to prove for 20 minutes, then bake for 10–15 minutes.

Meanwhile heat the oil in a saucepan and gently fry the chopped onions and garlic for 10 to 15 minutes, taking care that they do not colour. Stir in the tomato purée, tomatoes and herbs. Season well and let the mixture simmer uncovered for a further 20 minutes, so that the flavours blend together and a rich juicy sauce is formed.

Spread this sauce over the top of the pizza base, cover with grated cheese and any of the suggested garnishes. Reduce the oven temperature to gas mark 6, 400°F (200°C) and bake the pizza for 20 to 25 minutes until the cheese is golden brown on top and the pizza is thoroughly heated through. Serve hot or cold.

SESAME SABLÉS

This is a traditional recipe for melt-in-the-mouth rich cheese biscuits using Cheddar or Lancashire cheese. I add sesame seeds to them as I think it gives a good crunchy texture. They make a good accompaniment to soups and buffet salads.

Makes approximately 24–30 biscuits
3 oz (75 g) wholewheat flour
3 oz (75 g) butter
3 oz (75 g) grated cheese
1 tablespoon sesame seeds
salt and freshly ground black pepper
1 egg, lightly beaten
extra sesame seeds for topping

Pre-heat the oven to gas mark 5, 375°F (190°C).

Put the flour into a bowl, cut in the butter and then rub it in lightly. Add the cheese and sesame seeds and season well. Press the mixture together to form a dough, then wrap it in greaseproof paper and chill for half an hour.

Roll out the dough on a floured board into an oblong about $\frac{1}{4}$ inch (0·5 cm) thick. Keep the rolling pin and board well dusted with flour as it tends to be sticky. Cut the dough into strips 2 inches (5 cm) wide, brush with beaten egg and sprinkle with sesame seeds. Then cut them into triangle shapes. Place the biscuits on greaseproof paper on a baking sheet and bake for 10 minutes until they are golden brown. When cooked, lift the greaseproof paper onto a cool surface so the biscuits cool quickly. Store in an air-tight container.

BRAZILIAN CROUSTADE

My version of a croustade is a base made from breadcrumbs, cheese and nuts bound together with some oil. It can be baked well in advance and then re-heated when the topping is added. I use it for all sorts of plain and fancy vegetable toppings and vary the base by using different nuts or cheeses. This version is covered with a dark-coloured, spicy mushroom sauce so a bright green garnish of fresh parsley adds the right touch of colour.

Serves 4
4 oz (110 g) Brazil nuts
4 oz (110 g) grated Cheddar cheese
6 oz (175 g) fresh breadcrumbs
2 tablespoons oil
1 lb (450 g) mushrooms, wiped and sliced
3 oz (75 g) butter
8 oz (225 g) black-eyed or haricot beans, cooked and mashed
$\frac{1}{4}$ onion, peeled and grated
1 clove garlic, crushed
$\frac{1}{2}$ teaspoon chilli powder
1 tablespoon water
4 fl oz (110 ml) red wine
salt and freshly ground black pepper

Garnish:
1 tablespoon fresh parsley, finely chopped

Pre-heat the oven to gas mark 5, 375°F (190°C).

Chop the Brazil nuts coarsely and mix them with the cheese and breadcrumbs in a bowl. Mix in the oil to make a soft crumble-type texture. Grease a baking dish 11 × 7 inches (28 × 18 cm) and press in the breadcrumb mixture. Bake for 15 minutes until brown.

Meanwhile prepare the sauce. Sauté the mushrooms for 3 minutes in the butter, then add the mashed beans, grated onion, garlic and chilli powder mixed with 1 tablespoon of water. Simmer for 10 minutes on a low heat, stirring occasionally. Remove the pan from the heat and add the wine, salt and freshly ground black pepper. Spoon this sauce over the cooked breadcrumb base and bake for 10 to 15 minutes until heated through. Garnish with fresh parsley.

VEGETABLE CROUSTADE

This croustade is very quick to make. I use almonds as the main nut ingredient for the base as they have a delicious milky flavour which enhances cream sauces. The vegetable filling is a combination of leeks, sprouts and red peppers so it has good colour and texture, but I've also had success with other combinations such as courgettes, green beans and red peppers or fresh peas, artichoke hearts and sweet baby carrots. The sauce for the vegetables should be made fairly thick so that when you serve the croustade you can cut it easily into wedges. If it is a little thin the excess liquid tends to soak into the base and make it soggy. However, if you like plenty of sauce make extra white sauce or use sour cream and yoghurt and hand this round separately. Serve hot with either baked potatoes or rice and a choice of salads.

Serves 4–6

For the base:
4 oz (110 g) almonds, unblanched
4 oz (110 g) grated Cheddar cheese
6 oz (175 g) fresh breadcrumbs
1 teaspoon mixed herbs
1 clove garlic, crushed
2 tablespoons oil

For the topping:
1 lb (450 g) vegetables—a mixture of leeks, Brussels sprouts and red pepper
1 oz (25 g) butter or 1 tablespoon oil for frying the vegetables
2 medium onions, peeled and finely chopped
1 clove garlic, crushed
2 tablespoons oil
4 oz (110 g) mushrooms, wiped and sliced
1 dessertspoon flour
½ teaspoon grated nutmeg
½ pint (275 ml) milk
salt and freshly ground black pepper
1 tablespoon soy sauce

Pre-heat the oven to gas mark 5, 375°F (190°C).

First prepare the base. Chop the almonds, leaving them fairly coarse, and mix them with the grated cheese and breadcrumbs in a large bowl. Add the herbs and garlic and mix in the oil to form a soft crumble-type texture. Press this into a greased round or deep oven-proof plate 11 × 7 inches (28 × 13 cm) and bake for 15 minutes.

Meanwhile make the topping. Wash the vegetables and chop them into small dice. Gently fry them in the butter or oil, then cover the pan and cook until soft, adding a little water if necessary. In a separate pan heat 2 tablespoons of oil and fry the onions and garlic for a few minutes. Then add the mushrooms. Cook the mixture for a further few minutes, then sprinkle in the flour and nutmeg and brown slightly. Next pour in the milk, stirring constantly, to make a sauce. Season well with salt, freshly ground black pepper and soy sauce and simmer for 5 minutes, stirring occasionally. Add the cooked vegetables to the sauce and mix together well. Spoon this sauce over the cooked base and bake for 20–25 minutes until the croustade is thoroughly hot. Serve immediately.

WHOLEWHEAT SCONES

It is now possible to buy self-raising wholewheat flour. This is ideal for scones which are quick to make, but which disappear even more quickly! They have a delicious nutty flavour and I usually bake one large round and cover it with sesame seeds. You can make several times this quantity as baked scones freeze well.

Makes 1 large round (approximately 8–10 portions)

1½ oz (40 g) butter or margarine
8 oz (225 g) self-raising wholewheat flour
pinch salt
2 oz (50 g) brown sugar
2–3 tablespoons sultanas
1 beaten egg plus enough milk to make ¼ pint (150 ml) liquid
1 teaspoon sesame seeds

Pre-heat the oven to gas mark 7, 425°F (220°C).

Rub the butter or margarine into the flour with salt. Add the sugar, sultanas and egg-milk mixture, reserving a little for a glaze. Mix well, then knead the mixture lightly on a floured board. Shape it into a large round and put it onto a greased baking tray. Brush the round with the remaining milk and sprinkle with sesame seeds. With a blunt knife, lightly mark out 8 or 10 wedges. Bake for 15–20 minutes. Lift on to a cooling rack and serve warm.

RICH BREAD RING

This savoury ring is made from a rich buttery dough and has a texture that is a cross between bread and cake. The dough is first rolled out flat and the filling then spread on top. Then the whole thing is rolled up and formed into a ring. Cutting the ring reveals alternate layers of bread and filling which look quite spectacular. I have given recipes for two delicious fillings. Serve this loaf for lunch parties or perhaps an after-theatre supper.

Makes 1 ring
9 oz (250 g) strong unbleached white flour
pinch salt
$\frac{1}{2}$ oz (10 g) fresh yeast or $\frac{1}{4}$ oz (5 g) dried yeast
$\frac{1}{2}$ oz (10 g) brown sugar
$3\frac{1}{2}$ fl oz (100 ml) milk
1 beaten egg
$\frac{1}{2}$ tablespoon oil
2 oz (50 g) butter

Pre-heat the oven to gas mark 6, 400°F (200°C).

Place the flour and salt in a bowl and put it in a warm place. Then cream together the yeast and sugar, so that it becomes liquid. Gently heat the milk until it is just warm and pour it over the yeast mixture, stirring it in well. Add the beaten egg and stir again. Leave the mixture to rest for 5 minutes in a warm place, then pour it over the flour and add the oil, stirring with a wooden spoon.

219

Turn the dough out onto a lightly floured board and knead well. Then lightly oil the surface, put it into a clean bowl and cover with a damp cloth. This helps to prevent a crust forming as the dough rises. Leave it in a warm place for about 1 hour until the dough has doubled in size.

Flour a board and roll the risen dough out into an oblong 4 × 12 inches (10 × 30 cm). Cover two-thirds of the dough with 1 oz (25 g) butter chopped into small pieces, and fold the dough by turning the bottom third over the centre and the top third over both. Seal the side edges and give the dough a quarter-turn clockwise. Roll it out and repeat with the remaining 1 oz (25 g) butter. Then wrap the dough in some lightly oiled greaseproof paper and chill in the refrigerator for 15 minutes while you make the filling.

ALMOND, CHEESE AND POPPY SEED FILLING

2 large onions, peeled and finely chopped
1 tablespoon oil
2 oz (50 g) blue poppy seeds
4 oz (110 g) ground almonds
2 oz (50 g) grated Cheddar cheese
1 beaten egg
salt and freshly ground black pepper
extra poppy seeds to decorate

Gently fry the onions in the oil until transparent, then remove them from the heat and mix in the remaining ingredients, keeping a little of the egg for glazing the finished loaf. Season the mixture well.

CREAM CHEESE AND PARSLEY FILLING

6 oz (175 g) cream cheese
1 tablespoon fresh parsley, finely chopped
a little egg for glazing the finished loaf
poppy seeds to decorate

Mix the cream cheese and parsley together in a bowl.

To finish the loaf, remove the dough from the refrigerator and fold and roll it a couple more times. Then roll it out into an oblong 14 × 8 inches (35 × 20 cm) and spread the filling over the dough. Turn the long side towards you and roll the dough up like a Swiss roll. Shape this into a ring, pinching the two ends together, then make 10 cuts around the ring, almost as though you're cutting wedges, as this allows the dough to expand well. Brush it with beaten egg and sprinkle the top thickly with poppy seeds. Place the ring on a greased baking sheet and leave to rise for 15–20 minutes. Bake for 30–35 minutes and serve warm or cold.

CORN BREAD MUFFINS

Corn breads are some of the most famous American speciality breads made with golden corn meal which is also known as maize flour or, in Italy, polenta. It has a distinctive yellow colour and sweet, nutty flavour. One of the ways of using this flour is in American spoon bread, which is a cross between a soufflé and a bread.

You should be able to find corn meal at good health food shops or under the name of polenta at a delicatessen or good supermarket. I like to use corn meal to make little buns or muffins for savouries, flavouring them with onion and cheese. They are popular either for a savoury snack or as a delicious accompaniment to soup. They can also be served with extra cheese and salads for a simple meal.

Makes 8–10 small buns
1 tablespoon olive oil
1 small onion, peeled and very finely chopped
3 oz (75 g) plain wholewheat flour
3 oz (75 g) corn meal
1½ teaspoons baking powder
½ teaspoon salt
1 small egg
1 dessertspoon clear honey
¼ pint (150 ml) milk
1½ oz (40 g) Cheddar or Edam cheese, grated

Pre-heat the oven to gas mark 6, 400°F (200°C).

Heat the oil in a small frying-pan and gently fry the onion until it is soft. Mix together the wholewheat flour and corn meal with the baking powder and salt in a small mixing bowl. In another bowl thoroughly beat the egg, then add the honey and milk and beat again. Stir the egg mixture into the flour and add the cooked onion with all the residue of olive oil. Mix this together well to make a batter with a soft 'dropping' consistency. Then add the grated cheese. Spoon small amounts of the batter into a greased bun tin and put them in the oven for 10–12 minutes until the buns are risen, golden brown on the top and firm to the touch. Serve straight away, or let them cool and re-heat gently before serving.

PUDDINGS and CAKES

Apricot Syllabub 🐝 Brown Bread Ice-cream 🐝 Carob and Orange Roulade
Fruit Crumble 🐝 Pears Alhambra 🐝 St Clement's Cream Cheesecake
Rum and Raisin Cheesecake 🐝 Cinnamon and Carrot Cake
Blue Poppy Seed Cake

I think that on the whole puddings are best regarded as a special treat. They can be lavish and creamy like Rum and Raisin Cheesecake or light and delicate like Carob and Orange Roulade, both of these being rather indulgent puddings which are particularly suitable for a special meal or dinner party. As all of us are aware these days, however, that for the sake of our health, figures and teeth, it is important not to over-indulge in rich, sweet foods. Enjoy them occasionally. This doesn't mean you have to give up puddings entirely. In this section I've included lots of other ideas for sweets which, though not rich, are just as delicious. My favourite of these is Fruit Crumble which is good served hot or cold. Other mouth-watering fruit recipes include Pears Alhambra, which is fresh pears stewed in red wine, and Apricot Syllabub which is made from dried apricots soaked in white wine and puréed with cream.

I've also included a couple of unusual cake recipes. Carrot cakes are standard wholefood fare and my version is spiced with cinnamon. It is a delicious alternative to Christmas cake. The Poppy Seed Cake is quite unusual and has a marvellous flavour and texture. I'm sure you'll find both of these popular additions to your tea-table.

APRICOT SYLLABUB

This is a mouth-watering dessert with the delicate flavour of apricots stewed in wine. Other dried fruits such as peaches, pears or prunes are delicious as an alternative.

Serves 4
4 oz (110 g) apricots soaked overnight in $\frac{1}{4}$ pint (150 ml) white wine
2 egg whites
1 oz (25 g) light raw cane sugar
juice of $\frac{1}{2}$ lemon
$\frac{1}{4}$ pint (150 ml) double cream, whipped

Decoration:
flaked almonds, toasted

Soak the apricots overnight in wine, then stew them gently in a covered pan for 20 minutes or until they are soft. Add up to $\frac{1}{4}$ pint (150 ml) of extra fruit juice or water if necessary. Let the fruit cool, then liquidise or sieve the apricots with some of the cooking liquid to obtain a smooth purée. Whisk the egg whites until stiff and then whisk in the sugar. Fold in the apricot purée, lemon juice and whipped cream. Pile the mixture into 4 attractive glasses, or small dishes. Chill for 3–4 hours. Decorate with a sprinkling of toasted flaked almonds.

BROWN BREAD ICE-CREAM

This is a marvellous ice-cream, easy to make and quick to freeze, which has a flavour similar to praline. It is also the best way I know of using up breadcrumbs. Serve it with the Pears Alhambra (page 228), a fruit salad, or Fruit Crumble (page 227).

Makes 1 pint (570 ml)
3 oz (75 g) fresh brown breadcrumbs
3 oz (75 g) demerara sugar
2 eggs, separated
1 tablespoon honey
$\frac{3}{4}$ pint (400 ml) double or whipping cream

Pre-heat the oven to gas mark 5, 375°F (190°C).

Mix the breadcrumbs and the sugar together and spread them out on a baking sheet. Bake until the sugar has melted and the breadcrumbs have caramelised. (This is like making praline.) Then let them cool completely.

Beat the egg yolks and honey in a large bowl. Next lightly whip the cream. Whisk the egg whites until they are firm but not dry. Fold the cream and egg whites together and then fold them carefully into the egg yolk and honey mixture. Stir in the caramelised breadcrumbs and freeze the mixture until firm. (This takes a few hours.) About 20 minutes before serving, take the ice-cream out of the freezer and stand it in the refrigerator, so that it softens slightly.

CAROB AND ORANGE ROULADE

Carob is a powder which comes from the carob or locust bean which dates back to the time of John the Baptist. It is an excellent substitute for chocolate or cocoa, as it tastes the same but is cheaper, does not contain caffeine and is not artificially sweetened. You can use carob powder for making cakes, puddings and hot drinks but be sure to dissolve it well, otherwise it can be grainy. Carob 'chocolate' and powder is available from wholefood shops and health stores. I think this is an attractive party sweet which is rich yet light.

Serves 4–6
4 eggs
4 oz (110 g) light raw cane sugar
$\frac{1}{4}$ pint (150 ml) milk
2–3 tablespoons carob powder
grated rind of 2 oranges
$7\frac{1}{2}$ fl oz (200 ml) double cream
$\frac{1}{2}$ teaspoon vanilla essence
rind and juice of 1 orange
Decoration:
icing sugar
extra whipped cream

Pre-heat the oven to gas mark 4, 350°F (180°C).

Grease and line one 8 × 12 inch (20·5 × 30·5 cm) Swiss roll tin. Separate the eggs and whisk the yolks and sugar until they are pale and fluffy. Mix the carob powder and milk in a small saucepan and stir over a gentle heat until the carob powder has dissolved and the mixture thickens. Leave it to get cold, then whisk it into the egg yolks together with the grated rind of 2 oranges. Beat the egg whites until they are stiff and fold them into the carob mixture. Spread this evenly over the Swiss roll tray and bake it for 17 minutes until it has risen and is just firm.

Turn the roulade out onto a clean sheet of greaseproof paper and cover it with a warm damp cloth to stop it from drying out. Chill for 20 minutes.

Meanwhile whip the cream with the vanilla essence and fold in the rind and juice of 1 orange. Spread this over the roulade and then roll it up carefully. Don't try to roll it too tightly and don't worry if it cracks slightly. Dust it with icing sugar and if you like, pipe on extra cream. Serve chilled.

FRUIT CRUMBLE

I like to use combinations of fresh and dried fruits when making fruit crumbles. Mixtures such as dates and apples, dried peaches and fresh pears, rhubarb and figs, or raisins and oranges are all delicious. The topping can be a plain mixture of flour, oats and fat, using demerara sugar to give a crunchy quality, or varied by adding chopped nuts such as walnuts or coconut or sesame seeds. Serve this with ice-cream, custard or cream.

Serves 4–6

For the filling:
6 oz (175 g) dried apricots, washed
½ pint (275 ml) water or fruit juice
2 large bananas, sliced

For the topping:
2 oz (50 g) butter or margarine
3 oz (75 g) plain wholewheat flour
3 oz (75 g) porridge oats
2 oz (50 g) demerara sugar
4 tablespoons oil (preferably sunflower oil)

Pre-heat the oven to gas mark 4, 350°F (180°C).

Soak the apricots in water or fruit juice overnight, or bring them to the boil and simmer them gently in a covered pan until they are soft. Drain and reserve the juice. Put the apricots in a lightly greased ovenproof dish and mix in the banana slices. Pour in enough juice to cover the fruit.

Prepare the topping. Rub the fat into the flour, then mix in the oats, sugar and oil. Sprinkle the topping over the fruit and bake the crumble for 20–25 minutes until it is well browned. Serve hot.

227

PEARS ALHAMBRA

This is a light dessert which is always popular. When pears are stewed in red wine they turn a beautiful rosy colour which looks very attractive. This is delicious served with the Brown Bread Ice-cream (page 225).

Serves 4
4 pears (preferably Williams or Comice)
grated rind of 1 orange
½ pint (275 ml) sweet red wine
1 tablespoon crystallised ginger, finely chopped
1 oz (25 g) demerara sugar

Peel the pears, leaving the stalks on if possible, and slice a small portion from the base so that they will stand upright. Bring the wine to the boil with the orange rind. Add the peeled pears and poach them gently for 20 minutes. Remove them from the pan and stand them in a serving dish. Boil the remaining juice with the crystallised ginger and sugar until it thick and syrupy, then spoon it carefully over the pears. Chill thoroughly and serve with cream or ice-cream.

ST CLEMENT'S CREAM CHEESECAKE

There are two ways of making the topping for this cheesecake, one using traditional dairy products and one using Silken Tofu, a creamy substance made from the curds and whey of the soya bean. It is flavoured with orange and lemon juice and set with agar–agar. Agar–agar is the most commonly available vegetable gelatine which can be bought from health food stores or wholefood shops. Be sure to blend it thoroughly into the mixture, otherwise the end result will be grainy. I think it is essential to have a liquidiser or food processor for this recipe.

Makes 1 × 8 inch (20·5 cm) round cheesecake

For the base
---
3 oz (75 g) butter or margarine

1½ oz (40 g) brown sugar
---
3 oz (75g) plain wholewheat flour
---
3 oz (75 g) porridge oats

For the topping:
---
2 × 10½ oz (297 g) packets Silken Tofu (see page 205) or 12 oz (350 g) mixed cheeses—½ cream cheese, ½ curd cheese
---
4 tablespoons maple syrup
---
grated rind of 1 lemon and 1 orange
---
2 teaspoons agar–agar (see page 18)
---
juice of 2 oranges
---
juice of 1 lemon

Decoration:
---
zest of 1 orange

¼ pint (150 ml) whipped cream

Pre-heat the oven to gas mark 4, 350°F (180°C).

First prepare the base. Cream together the butter and sugar. Add the flour and oats and beat them together thoroughly. Press this mixture into a greased flan tin 8 inches (20·5 cm) in diameter, preferably loose-bottomed. Bake for 15 minutes until it is firm and well browned.

Meanwhile make the topping. Put the tofu, maple syrup, lemon and orange rind in a liquidiser and blend them thoroughly until they are smooth. If using the mixed cheeses, beat these with the maple syrup, lemon and orange rind until well blended. Check the sweetening. Put the agar–agar with the orange and lemon juice into a small pan and bring gently to the boil. Let it cool slightly, then pour it into the tofu or cheese mixture and blend together thoroughly. Leave the mixture to cool, stirring occasionally, and when it is almost at setting point, pour it over the prepared base. Chill the cake for 3–4 hours or overnight until it is completely firm. Decorate the cheesecake with grated orange zest and whipped cream.

RUM AND RAISIN CHEESECAKE

This rich cheesecake definitely belongs in the special treats category. I like to flavour it with raisins soaked in rum but you could use other dried fruit and liqueur/spirit combinations.

Makes 1 × 8 inch (20·5 cm) round cheesecake

For the base:
4 oz (110 g) butter or margarine
2 oz (50 g) brown sugar
3 oz (75 g) plain wholewheat flour
3 oz (75 g) ground almonds

For the topping:
2 eggs, separated
2 oz (50 g) light raw cane sugar
6 oz (175 g) cream cheese
6 oz (175 g) curd cheese
½ teaspoon vanilla essence
4 oz (110 g) raisins soaked in 3 tablespoons rum
¼ pint (150 ml) double cream

Pre-heat the oven to gas mark 4, 350°F (180°C).

First make the base. Cream the fat and sugar until they are light and fluffy. Then stir in the flour and ground almonds and beat the mixture to make a dough. Press the dough into an 8 inch (20·5 cm) round greased cake tin, preferably one with a loose, removable base. Bake for 15 minutes until the base is brown and well cooked.

Meanwhile prepare the filling. Beat the egg yolks with 1 oz (25 g) of the sugar, then beat in the cheeses, vanilla essence and soaked raisins and rum. Whip the cream and fold it into the mixture. Whisk the egg whites until they are stiff and beat in the remaining 1 oz (25 g) sugar. Fold the egg whites carefully into the cheese mixture. Spoon the filling over the cooled base and chill the cheesecake for 4–5 hours or overnight until it has set.

OPPOSITE:
Carob and Orange Roulade (*page 226*)
Apricot Syllabub (*page 224*)
Pears Alhambra (*page 228*)
Brown Bread Ice-cream (*page 225*)

CINNAMON AND CARROT CAKE

There are recipes dating from the Roman times in which carrots were used for their sweetness and colour. I've come across many cakes and puddings which use them, including a recipe entitled 'King George IV Christmas Pudding'. The cake given here has a rich colour and close texture, and it is heavily spiced with cinnamon and nutmeg. It will freeze or keep well for several days in an air-tight tin. Serve it with morning coffee or as a special cake for a picnic lunch.

Makes 1 × 1 lb (450 g) cake
½ lb (225 g) plain wheatmeal or wholewheat flour
1 tablespoon cinnamon
1 teaspoon nutmeg
½ tablespoon baking powder
4 oz (110 g) butter or margarine
4 oz (110 g) honey
4 oz (110 g) sugar
½ lb (225 g) carrots, peeled and finely grated

Pre-heat the oven to gas mark 3, 325°F (170°C).

Mix together the flour, spices and baking powder in a large bowl. Then melt the butter, honey and sugar together in a saucepan, and stir this mixture into the flour, combining all ingredients thoroughly. Next stir in the grated carrots. Put the mixture into a well greased 1 lb (450 g) loaf tin and bake for 60–80 minutes, until it feels firm to the touch and a skewer inserted into the centre comes out clean. Leave the cake in the tin for 10 minutes, then turn it out onto a cooling rack.

OPPOSITE:
Cinnamon and Carrot Cake (*above*)
Blue Poppy Seed Cake (*page 234*)

BLUE POPPY SEED CAKE

This is a delicious cake for coffee time or afternoon tea. Poppy seeds are sold in wholefood stores, health shops and many supermarkets, and they are cheapest when sold loose. They are mainly used in this country for decorating bread, but in Eastern European countries they are also used in sweet pastry fillings and cakes. In this recipe the poppy seeds give a lovely texture and subtle flavour to the cake. It can be frozen, or will keep well in an air-tight container.

Makes 1 × 8 inch (20·5 cm) cake

4 oz (110 g) blue poppy seeds
8 fl oz (225 ml) milk
8 oz (225 g) butter or margarine
8 oz (225 g) light raw cane sugar
3 eggs, separated
8 oz (225 g) plain wheatmeal flour
1¼ teaspoons baking powder

Pre-heat the oven to gas mark 4, 350°F (180°C).

Line and grease an 8 inch (20·5cm) cake tin. Bring the poppy seeds to the boil in the milk, then turn off the heat and let them soak for 25 minutes in a covered pan. Meanwhile cream the butter and sugar together until light and fluffy. Add the egg yolks, one at a time, and beat them in thoroughly. Mix the flour and baking powder together and fold this into the creamed mixture. Then stir in the soaked poppy seeds and milk. Next, whisk the egg whites until they are stiff and fold them in carefully. Spoon the mixture into the prepared tin and bake the cake for 1 hour or until the centre feels firm and a skewer when inserted into the cake comes out clean. Let the cake stand in the tin for 10 minutes, then turn it on to a cooling rack.

FURTHER INFORMATION

FURTHER READING

DAVID, E. *English bread and yeast cookery* Allen Lane, 1977;
Penguin Books, 1979.
ROBERTSON, L. *et al. Laurel's kitchen: a handbook for vegetarian
cookery and nutrition* Routledge and Kegan Paul, 1979.
SINGER, P. *Animal liberation* Thorsons, 1983.
THOMAS, A. *The vegetarian epicure* Penguin Books, 1973.
WRIGHT, H. *Swallow it whole: the New Statesman's survival guide to
the food industry* New Statesman, 1983.

MAIL ORDER FOR WHOLEFOOD AND VEGETARIAN INGREDIENTS

Clearspring Mail Order (UK only), 196 Old Street,
London EC1V 9BP (Tel: 01-250 1708).

INFORMATION ON VEGETARIANISM

The Vegetarian Society, Parkdale, Dunham Road, Altrincham,
Cheshire WA14 4QG (Tel: 061-928 0793), *or* 53 Marloes Road,
London W8 6LD (Tel: 01-937 7739).

INDEX